The Greenleaf Guide to
Famous Men of
The Middle Ages

by Cyndy A. Shearer
& Robert G. Shearer

Greenleaf Press
Lebanon, Tennessee

© 1992, Greenleaf Books, LLC

Published by
Greenleaf Books, LLC
Sixth Printing, June 2006

Internet: www.greenleafpress.com
3761 Highway 109N, Unit D
Lebanon, Tennessee 37087
615-449-1617

History for the thoughtful child

Introduction

When you want to build something, a hammer is a very useful thing to have. But if someone picks up your hammer and starts beating you over the head with it, the hammer is no longer a tool — it's a murder weapon. So it is with textbooks and study guides. Used correctly, they are useful tools — but don't let anyone use them as a weapon to beat you up with a rigid list of "how you should be doing it..." Like all Greenleaf Guides, this book is intended to be used as a tool, a possible model for you to use and adapt as you see fit. You will know what suggestions will work best for the students you teach, and you should feel free to make the course fit your family's needs.

The Study Guide is designed to be used with the <u>Famous Men of the Middle Ages</u> text. It also makes suggestions for other readings from various fiction and non-fiction sources and provides lists of vocabulary and a list of the places and people mentioned in each chapter. We have also included possible discussion questions for each chapter. Some of them may be useful starting points for written assignments, but for the most part, they are intended merely as a guide to the teacher — as a starting point for discussion rather than "questions found at the end of the chapter, to be answered by the students by copying passages from the text." If your high school experience was anything like ours, you probably have the same negative reaction to that style of teaching that we do.

A word about discussion: in our family study we have begun using narration as a beginning point for our discussions. I commend the practice to you. It is one of the basic building blocks of the Charlotte Mason approach. Here is the way she describes it:

> "As knowledge is not assimilated until it is reproduced, children should "tell back" after a single reading or hearing: or should write on some part of what they have read. A **single reading** is insisted on, because children have naturally great power of attention; but this force is dissipated by the re-reading of passages, and also, by questioning, summarizing , and the like. (<u>A Philosophy of Education</u>, introduction.)"

In summary, we read or they read the passage once and then tell it back to us. As they are narrating, we try not to comment — unless there is some gross misunderstanding that prevents further understanding. Any background material — such as map skills, or definitions of words expected to be problematic — should be given before the reading so that they will be able to read with understanding the first time through. Then they tell me what they have just read. At first there were lots of long empty pauses, and looks that begged for rescue. But each week has brought marked improvement. The reason that Miss Mason says not to ask questions as they go along, is that the practice interferes with their own internal "ordering" of the material. If they know you will be asking them the questions, they will wait for you to tell them what they need to remember. If left alone, they have to ask themselves the questions, and learn to identify significant details and events. I have found that beginning our discussion with narration, we take care of the more obvious observation questions that can become so stilted and tedious. Then we can concentrate on the questions that force the child to interpret and apply his own prior stores of knowledge to the new material — evaluating and criticizing. In this setting the discussion questions merely suggest primary themes, issues, points of view that are central to the chapter and probably should be dealt with in some fashion. Please resist the temptation to approach the discussion questions as if they were a catechism.

A Note on multi-level teaching:

If you are using this material for older students, eighth grade and up, you may find that you can have these students incorporate high school level literature selections into their study. The older high school students can be reading Beowulf and Chaucer while the younger students are reading selections from the children's fiction set in the Middle Ages. For instance, younger children might read selections from Canterbury Tales, written for children while the high school students reads selections from the original.

A Note on testing:

When we think of testing, we usually think of exams — essay questions, true/false, multiple choice. There is a place for traditional testing both in and out of conventional classroom settings, but don't overlook the other options. If after reading a story, or listening to you read it aloud, the child is able to tell you the story in his own words — you can know that he understands it. That's really the reason for testing... to make sure your student understands the material.

Another means by which you can evaluate a student's understanding of a selection is through oral discussion. As stated earlier, the "For Discussion" questions provided for each chapter are intended to be suggestions — questions you might ask. Often, as you discuss the reading, you will naturally cover the material without sticking to a rigid "question/answer" format. Treasure those times! Sometimes you will need to draw your students along point by point. Sometimes you will need to ask questions different from those suggested. By all means, do.

Written assignments also help evaluate understanding. Some "For Discussion" questions will work particularly well as essay topics. Occasionally have your students retell the story by presenting it as a news story, short story, play, etc.

Suggestions for Teacher Preparation:

1. Familiarize yourself with the timeline at the back of the study guide, so that you have a sense of where you are going to begin and end. This will also briefly introduce you to the names of some of the people you will be reading about.

2. Read through the study guide's lessons and the assignments before you begin teaching them. Decide which activities you will do with which children, and which additional readings you will assign. Most of the books suggested in the guide make excellent family read aloud choices.

Books Used in This Study:

This study guide makes use of the following books — as of this writing all are in print. As in other guides, occasional references are made to back issues of <u>National Geographic Magazine,</u> and other videos. Public Libraries and used books stores may also have books that you may find useful. One of the most disheartening things about the book business is that many excellent works of historical fiction written for children go out of print every year. They come into print in hardback, do not sell well enough to warrant reprinting in more affordable paperback editions and are thus discontinued. Keep your eyes open and you will probably stumble onto some real treasures.

Primary Texts:

<u>Famous Men of the Middle Ages</u>, Greenleaf Press, 1992

<u>The New Penguin Atlas of Medieval History</u>, Penguin Books, 1992

<u>Cathedral</u>, David Macaulay, Houghton Mifflin, 1973

<u>Castle</u>, David Macaulay, Houghton Mifflin, 1977

Supplemental Texts:

The Middle Ages is an incredibly rich period, and one that seems to stir our imaginations. We feel like use of the four primary texts listed above will provide you with a thorough study of the period, however, we really recommend that you add some of the following books to your study. Most are in print, some (marked with an **, are not). Most should be available at your local library.

<u>D'aulaires' Norse Gods and Giants</u>, Doubleday, 1967
<u>The Children of Odin</u>, Padraic Colum, Macmillan, 1952
The music of Wagner
<u>Charlemagne</u>, Einhard
<u>The Arabian Knights</u>
<u>Beowulf</u>, A verse translation by Frederick Rebsamen, HarperCollins, 1991
<u>The Story of the Champions of the Round Table</u>, Howard Pyle, Dover, 1968 reprint of the
      1905 edition
<u>Sir Gawain and the Green Knight</u>, trans by J.R.R. Tolkien, Ballantine, 1975
<u>Saint Patrick's Day</u>, Joyce K. Kessel, Carolrhoda Books, 1982

The Usborne Time Traveler Book of Viking Raiders, Usborne, 1990
Make This Viking Settlement, Usborne Cut-out Model, 1988
The Vikings, Elizabeth Janeway, Landmark/Random House, 1951
Beorn the Proud, Madalaine Polland**
The Black Fox of Lorne, Marguerite de Angeli**
A Tournament of Knights, Joe Lasker, Harper Trophy, 1986
Design Your Own Coat of Arms, Dover Press
MacBeth, William Shakespeare
"The Bayeaux Tapestry," National Geographic, August 1966
Otto of the Silver Hand, Howard Pyle, Dover Press, 1967 reprint of the 1888 edition
Adam of the Road, Elizabeth Janet Gray, Puffin Books, 1942
The Door in the Wall, Marguerite de Angeli, Dell Yearling, 1949
Living in Castle Times, Usborne, 1982
The Truth About Castles, Gillian Clements, Carolrhoda, 1988-1990
Time Traveller Book of Knights and Castles, Usborne, 1976
A Medieval Feast, Aliki, Harper Trophy, 1983
The Minstrel in the Tower, Gloris Skurzynski, Random House, 1988
The Magna Charta, James Daugherty, Landmark Book by Random House**
The Travels of Marco Polo
Marco Polo, Landmark Book by Random House**
Chanticleer and the Fox, Chaucer, illus. by Barbara Cooney, Harper Trophy, 1958
The Canterbury Tales, illus. by Trina Schart Hyman, Lothrop, Lee, & Shepherd, 1988
Henry V, William Shakespeare
Fine Print, Joann Johansen Burch, Carolrhoda, 1991
Ink on His Fingers, Louise Vernon, Greenleaf Press, 1993
Richard II, William Shakespeare
Henry V, William Shakespeare
Richard III, William Shakespeare
Cultural Atlas of the Middle Ages, Facts on File, 1990**

Rob & Cyndy Shearer

There are many more. Many of these books are available directly from Greenleaf Press. Please visit our web-site for more information.

Greenleaf Press
3761 Highway 109 N.
Lebanon, TN 37087
Phone: 615-449-1617
Email: info@greenleafpress.com
Web-Site: www.greenleafpress.com

Introduction I & II

The Gods of the Teutons
The Ring of the Niebelung

Vocabulary:

dialects	waft	brandish
routed	burnished	mead
abyss		
gain the mastery	forfeit	

People and Places:

Danube	Rhine	Goths
Vandals	Huns	Franks
Anglo-Saxons	Teutons	Woden/Odin
Sleipnir	Tiew	Attila
Frija	Thor	Baldur
Loki	Valkyries	Valhalla
Ymir	Ginnungagap	Nornes
Niebelungenlied	Siegfried	Siegmund
Kriemhilda	King Gunther	Worms
Balumng	Hagen	Iceland
Wagner		

Introduction I & II
The Gods of the Teutons & The Ring of the Niebelung
(continued)

For Discussion:

1. Who were the major gods worshipped by the Teutons? With what was each associated? Complete the "Matching Exercise," on page 10.

2. If you have studied the mythology of ancient Greece or Rome, you will probably notice some differences in the mythologies. How would you describe the gods worshipped by the ancient Greeks? How would you describe the Teutonic gods? What interests each group? Whom does each group of gods honor? Why is honor bestowed? Record your answers on the chart on page 11.

3. Like all cultures, the Germanic tribes had stories that describe the world's beginning and its end. What do these stories have in common with the biblical accounts? How do they differ? Record your answers on the chart on page 12.

4. C.S. Lewis and J.R.R. Tolkein loved the Norse Myths. These tales fed their imaginations. You might read more of Norse mythology in <u>D'aulaires' Book of Norse Gods and Heroes</u> or Padraic Colum's <u>The Children of Odin</u>. Your library may have other books, as well. (Don't forget to look in the picture book collection for illustrated re-tellings of Norse myths.)

5. You might listen to selections from Wagner's operas. The strong of heart might even take on a whole opera. Those whose weak stomachs prevent them from lasting through an entire opera should at least listen to "The Flight of the Valkyries," as it is probably the most well-known piece. After you have read some of the tales and listened to the music, ask your student(s) how well they think the music fits the tales.

6. You might study the life of Wagner. Why did the stories from Norse mythology interest him? The Music of the Masters tape series by Moss Music has a cassette entitled, "Wagner: His Life and Music." The story of the composer's life is told while selections from his music play in the background.

7. While you are studying the Vikings, you and your students might enjoy reading the comic strip "Hagar the Horrible." (At least Hagar doesn't sing soprano.)

Matching Exercise

a. Wodin/Odin

1. a frost giant

b. Ymir

2. beautiful female warriors

c. Baldur

3. Odin's horse

d. Sleipnir

4. the great abyss

e. Tiew

5. wife of Odin, Queen of gods

f. Thor

6. spirit of evil, Baldur's enemy

g. Frija

7. where the Valkyries take fallen warriors when they die in battle.

h. Valkyries

8. King of the gods

i. Ginnungagap

9. the favorite of the gods

j. Valhalla

10. son of Odin, god of battle

k. Loki

11. son of Odin, god of thunder.

Story of...	. . . in Teutonic mythology	. . . in Biblical accounts
Creation of the World		
The End of the World		

	Teutonic Myths	Greek Myths	Bible
Characteristics of the gods/God			
What they value			
Who they honor			
What they honor			
Man's purpose for living			

Chapter I

Alaric the Visigoth

Other Resources:

Penguin Atlas, pages 12-13 and page 14-15 show the route of Alaric and the Visigoths on their journey from east to west through the Empire.

Vocabulary:

pillage   gladiators

People and Places:

Romania	Constantinople	Valens
Bulgaria	Alaric	Eastern Illyricum
Honorius	Stilicho	Western Illyricum
Epirus	Ionian Sea	

For Discussion:

1. Why did Emperor Valens attack the Goths' land? How was this conflict resolved?

2. Why did the Goths come to Valens later? What did they ask of him? How did Valens respond?

3. Finish the following statements:

   Visigoths were Goths who came from the _____.

   Ostrogoths were Goths who came from the _____.

4. Who was Alaric? How would you describe him? Why?

5. Describe Alaric's dream. How did he react to it? What was the end result?

6. Tell what happened between Honorius and Alaric. What do you think of Honorius? Of Alaric? What do you think God would say about each man?

Chapter II

Attila the Hun

Other Resources:

Penguin Atlas, pages 16-17 show the empire of Attila.

Vocabulary:

vast	plot	enraged
scourge	majestic aspect	ransom
barbarous		

People and Places:

Emperor Theodosius	Germany	Gaul
Orleans	Plain of Champagne	Chalons
Aetius	Thorismond	Aquileis
Adriatic Sea	Venice	the "Hermit of the Rocks"

For Discussion:

1. Where did the Goths and the Huns originally live? Where did they move?

2. Describe Attila. Would you call him a wise man? Why or why not?

3. Why didn't Attila attack Rome? Explain this. What are some reasons that might possibly explain his withdrawal?

4. How did the Huns mourn Attila? What does the Bible have to say about this practice? (cf. Deuteronomy 14:1)

Chapter III

Genseric the Vandal

Other Resources:

Penguin Atlas, pages 18-19 show the kingdom of the Vandals under Genseric.

For High School and above: The Confessions, Saint Augustine

Vocabulary:

wanton	resolved	ravages
pirates	ambassador	suppress
expedition	truce	cautiously
cunning		

People and Places:

Baltic	Genseric	Count Boniface
Valentinian III	Placidia	Strait of Gibraltar
Hippo	Carthage	Eudoxia
Maximus	Tiber	Majorian
Basilicus	Bay of Carthagena	

For Discussion:

1. Describe the conflict between Boniface, Aetius and Placidia.

2. How did Genseric end up in Africa? What did he hope to accomplish there?

3. Why did Boniface change his mind about Genseric?

4. Describe Genseric's African campaign. Where did he fight? How did he behave? Who joined him and why did they join him?

5. Tell how Genseric came to Rome. Why did he go and what did he do while he was there? ("Pussy Cat, Pussy Cat, where have you been?...)

6. Tell how Majorian planned to punish Genseric and his pirates. How successful was he? Tell what happened.

7. Genseric was a very successful leader — what kind of man do you think he was? Would you enjoy spending time with someone like him? Explain your answer. Do you think God would describe him as successful? Again, explain your answer and be specific.

Chapter IV

Theodoric the Ostrogoth

Other Resources:

Penguin Atlas, pages 20-21 show the kingdom of the Ostrogoths under Theoderic.

Vocabulary:

patrician   hostages   sole

People and Places:

Odoacer   Emperor Zeno   Theodoric
Black Sea   Alps   Italy

For Discussion:

1. Describe Theodoric's upbringing. In what ways did it prepare him for the situations he would face in adulthood?

2. Tell about Theodoric's conquest of Italy. Why did he want to conquer the country? What did he want to do with it? Who was his major opponent? What was he like?

3. How would you compare Theodoric and Odoacer? Could you say, "The best man won?" Why or why not?

Chapter V

Clovis

Other Resources:

Penguin Atlas, pages 20-21 show the kingdom of the Franks under Clovis.

Vocabulary:

pious   fervent   dynasty

People and Places:

Clovis   Childeric   Syagrius
Clotilde   Cologne   Pyrenees
Merovengian Dynasty

For Discussion:

1. Find the Frankish kingdom on the map (page 20-21 in the Penguin Atlas of Medieval History).

2. How old was Clovis when he became king of the Franks? What kind of leader did he prove to be?

3. Tell the story of Clovis' campaign against Rome. What factors do you think contributed to Rome's defeat? How might Proverbs 16:18 apply to the situation?

4. Tell about Clovis and Clotilde. In what ways did Clotilde influence Clovis?

5. Tell about Clovis' conversion to Christianity.

Chapter VI

Justinian the Great

Other Resources:

Penguin Atlas, pages 26-27 show the Eastern Empire and the territory it re-conquered under Justinian.

Vocabulary:

dominion   mosque

People and Places:

Constantinople   Justinus I   Belisarius
Narses   Justinian   Gelimer
Code of Justinian

Discussion:

1. Find the kingdom of the Goths on the map.

2. Tell about Justinus' relationship with his Uncle Justin. What was Justinus like — describe his interests, abilities, etc.

3. How did the poor shepherd boy become Emperor of Rome?

4. Tell about Belsarius' campaign against the Vandal king, Gelimer. How was Belsarius received by the people of Africa? Why was this so?

5. Why do you think Justinian would want to drive the Ostrogoths out of Italy?

6. What was significant about the Code of Justinian?

7. Justinian is known in history as "Justinian the Great." Why do you think this is so? Do you think he deserves the title? Explain.

Chapter VI
Justinian the Great
(continued)

8. Mosaics were often used to decorate the walls and ceilings of churches and other structures during this period. You might want to take some time and study this art medium in more detail. Your students can make their own mosaic pictures in one of two ways.

The Easy Way...

Have your students either cut or tear different colored construction paper into little pieces (oh, joy!). These pieces can be uniform in size and/or shape, or they can be of a more randomly ripped design. Have your students make a rough sketch of their subject and let them "color" it by gluing the little pieces into the outlines.

The Other Way...

It is possible to purchase tile squares from Art Supply Companies or from companies that manufacture or sell tile to contractors. The second option is usually cheaper — in that you get more tile for your money but often more difficult to track down. The varieties of tile available may be greater, since what they are most likely to sell are "left-overs," but you may have to buy bigger quantities.

Nasco (901 Janesville Ave., Fort Atkinson, WI 53538 or call (414)563-2446) sells materials you would need to make a tile top for a small wooden box (knick-knack or jewelry box for a Christmas present for a Grandparent, perhaps). This may be the better option for a small scale project. NOTE: *Because you will need the tiles to fit into different sized and shaped spaces within your design, a good pair of tile cutters really help!*

Chapter VII

Benedict and Gregory

Other Resources:

Life in a 15th-Century Monastery, Anne Boyd, 1979, Lerner Publications, Minneapolis, MN.

Audio tape recordings or CDs of Gregorian Chants: "A Sacred Christmas," contains the chants as well as pieces by J.S. Bach. This particular tape is beautiful — but there are others around as well. Check with your local library for other listings.

Vocabulary:

monastery	monk	poverty
chastity	obedience	code of law
prefect	abbot	plague
monastic (life)	promote	convert
administer	efficient	Gregorian chant

People and Places:

Benedict	Gregory	Vatican
Europe		

For Discussion:

1. Tell about Benedict — what was his background? Why did he flee Rome?

2. Tell how the hermit came to rule a monastery. In what ways would monastic life differ from life in Rome? Why do you think the three vows required of the Benedictine monks concerned poverty, chastity and obedience?

3. Tell about Gregory. Describe his background. How did Gregory come to join the Benedictines? In what ways did he serve there?

4. Tell about his response to the plague. How did he behave/react? What does his behavior tell you about his character?

5. Once Gregory became Pope, what did he do?

Chapter VII
Benedict and Gregory
(continued)

6.   Listen to some Gregorian chants. Can you understand the words? What language were they written in? Why is this? What do you notice about the sound? How do the chants compare with today's church music? When you listen to this music, how does it make you feel? (If your support group is willing, you might even try singing some Gregorian chants together. Check with a local music store about available sheet music. Don't be surprised if you have to 1. Spell "Gregorian Chant" for the clerk; 2. Ask them to make a special order for you; 3. Answer the question, "What do you want this stuff for?" Then again, you may get lucky.

7.   Your family or support group might want to try keeping the monastic hours for one day. The schedule (according to St. Benedict's Rule) ran roughly as follows:

Midnight	*Matins* (the start of the new day) 1 hour
6 am	*Prime* 30 minutes (followed by Breakfast)
9 am	*Chapter Mass*
10 am	Chapter Meeting & Council
11 am	*High Mass* (followed by Dinner at Noon)
2 pm	*Nones* 30 minutes
4 pm	*Vespers* 30 minutes
6 pm	Supper
7 pm	*Compline* 30 minutes

Each of the Services (except the two Masses) consisted of hymns, psalms, Scripture readings, and readings from Christian writers (St. Augustine was reasonably popular).

Your sleepyheads may need encouragment to get up and get to the midnight service promptly. Here's how the monks did it:

If anyone was too late to come in the procession with the others he would have to come in alone and stretch himself out on the floor in the middle of the choir. This was a sign of apology for being late. The sub-prior would give a signal— probably a knock on the wood of his choir stall - and the latecomer could then get up and go to his place.

Life in a 15th-Century Monastery, p 18.

OR you might want to try eating a meal or two in monastic style. Meals were eaten in silence, with one monk appointed to read to the assembled chapter while they ate. The readings would include scripture as well as the writings of the Church fathers.

Chapter **VIII**

Mohammed

Other Resources:

Penguin Atlas, pages 32-33 shows the rise of Islam and its spread through North Africa and into Asia Minor.

Vocabulary:

Koran	imposter	doctrines
muezzin	enclosure	arcade
minaret	caliph	successor

People and places:

Islam	Mecca	Arabia
Mohammed	Red Sea	Khadijah
Mount Hira	Medina	Hejira

For Discussion:

1. Tell about Mohammed's family background. What was he known for among people who knew him?

2. In Luke 16:10 Jesus tells us that "He who is faithful in little will be faithful in much." How do you see this principle operating in Mohammed's life?

3. Tell how Mohammed came to write the Koran.

4. How does Islam compare with Christianity? Complete the chart on the next page. Reference specific Scriptures wherever you can.

5. Read Galatians 1:6-12. How do these verses apply to the Islamic religion?

6. Many of the people you have read about in this book have taken on adult responsibilities when they were only sixteen years old. Paul's friend and co-worker, Timothy was also a young man who was given great responsibilities. In I Timothy 4:12, Paul wrote Timothy, saying, "Let no man despise thy youth: but be thou an example of the believers, in word, in conversation, in charity and in spirit, in faith in purity." You might study the whole chapter for even more detail, but what does Paul mean by this? In what ways might you apply this to your own life?

Summary Sheet: Islam and Christianity

	Islam	Christianity
Who is Mohammed?		
Who is Jesus?		
How does a person please God?		
How should believers make disciples?		

Complete the chart after you have read "Mohammed." Use specific Scripture passages to support your summary statements.

Chapter IX

Charles Martel and Pepin

Other Resources:

Penguin Atlas, pages 34-35 show the Realm of the Franks under Charles Martel.

Vocabulary:

duties	throng	courtiers	assemblage	idle
decisive	consent (n)	temporal power	secular	

People and Places:

Saracens	Spain	Mayor of the Palace	Pepin
Charles Martel	Abder Rahmah	Pyrenees	Bordeaux
Tours	Poitiers		

For Discussion:

1. On a map, locate areas conquered by the Mohammedans (Saracens). What other areas did the Saracens intend to conquer?

2. Why were the Saracens so interested in extending their borders?

3. Describe the character of the French kings of this period. What were they interested in? Describe their duties. Describe the duties of the Mayor of the Palace. Compare the two.

4. Name two famous Mayors of the Palace. For what is each known?

5. Why was the name "Martel" given to Charles? What was significant about the battle of Tours?

6. Charles Martel had two sons (from this point on, Charles and Pepin become very popular names — try not to get confused). What were they like?

7. How did Pepin become king? What is meant by the term, "Pepin's Donation?" What was significant about it?

Chapter X

Charlemagne

Other Resources:

Penguin Atlas, pages 44-45 show the extent of the Carolingian Empire under Charlemagne.

Background Information:

As the Roman Empire fell apart, the various Germanic tribes moved in. With Charlemagne we see a period of political stability as law and order is restored. In addition, the Gospel was spread to many barbarian tribes. There was also a period of intellectual revival in which Greek and Roman manuscripts were copied and preserved.

Before you read the chapter, you might quickly lead your student/s through a review of Roman culture — its concern for reasonably uniform laws, the systems of roads that made it possible both to travel (by the standards of the day) quickly from place to place and to communicate with people and officials with some speed, and the ability to police the kingdom and see that laws were enforced uniformly. Rome also had a fairly broad economic base (that is, they were able to get money from many different sources). Talk about life after the Romans left the "frontiers." Talk about what it would take to enable one nation to successfully govern such a large region.

After your students have read the chapter, you might discuss reasons for the eventual dissolution of Charlemagne's Empire. A few suggestions follow.

Charlemagne's empire lacked strong administrative structures. It never developed the same sort of economic base that Rome had. There were no reliable systems of communication between regions, and they were unable to solve the problems associated with succession.

After Charlemagne's death in 814, his empire pretty much fell apart. By the time of Henry the Fowler (919-936), seven different kings ruled in place of one. The custom of dividing a kingdom among all legitimate heirs led to quarrels. Initially, Louis the Pious, Charles's only surviving son, inherited the kingdom. But when he died, his lands were divided between his three sons, Lothair, Louis and Charles the Bald. It wasn't long before civil war broke out among the brothers. In 843 Lothair was allowed to retain the title of emperor. He ruled the middle part of the Empire — the regions surrounding the Rhone, the Rhine and Italy. Charles the Bald took the western region and Louis ruled the eastern regions. You can imagine some of the long range effects of this practice. After your students have read and discussed the chapter, "Charlemagne," talk together about the reasons Charlemagne's empire did not survive him. Use the "Family Map" exercise (found on page 36) as a basis for your discussion. (The English avoided the problem, somewhat, by passing lands to the eldest son, occasionally, the eldest daughter).

Vocabulary:

civilized

Moorish

coat of mail

pomp

profess

People and Places:

Charlemagne

Alps

Moors

Western Roman Empire

Lothaire

Harun al Rashid

Wittekind

Damascus

Basques

Aix la Chapelle/Aachen

Charles

Lombards

Roland

Abder Rhaman

Louis

Alcuin

Discussion:

1. Pepin had two sons, Carloman and Charles (If this seems confusing, think of Carloman as Carl. Charlemagne is simply French for *Charles the Great* — Charles le Magne. We call him Charlemagne, his mother called him Charles.) How did Charles become king of France? What was he like? For more information, read Einhard's <u>Charlemagne</u>. Einhard was a faithful friend (and a bishop) of Charlemagne.

2. Tell about the Saxons. Find their kingdom on the map. What were they like? What influence did Charlemagne have on them?

3. Find the kingdom of the Lombards on the map. Why did Charlemagne attack the Lombards? How did he end up attacking the Damascus Moors in Spain? How successful was he in each campaign?

4. How did Charlemagne come to be called "Charles Augustus, Emperor of the Romans?"

5. Describe Charlemagne's attitude toward learning. In what ways did he attempt to further education in France?

6. Charlemagne's favorite proverb was "He that rules his spirit is better than he that takes a city." Explain what that means. What does that tell you about his character? Compare Charlemagne to Alexander the Great. How were they alike? How were they different? Would Alexander have liked Charlemagne's proverb?

Family Map Exercise

To demonstrate the effect that dividing a kingdom between all legitimate heirs had over time, use the map on the following page as the map of your family kingdom.

Step 1.   Say that your Dad is King. How many children are in your family? (In Charlemagne's time only the boys would inherit land — the girls would be married to men with holdings of their own. King Dad can choose to include daughters as well as sons in the list of legitimate heirs.)

Step 2.   If there are six children in your family, Dad will divide it up into six separate kingdoms. If there are two, there will be only two. How does Dad decide which land to give to which child? What if one child is dissatisfied with his piece? Divide the kingdom according to the number of children and write the heir's name in his or her respective piece.

Step 3.   Now Dad dies (sorry, Dad!). The siblings now rule their own kingdoms. They get married, have kids, and prepare to divide up their kingdoms. Say one has two children, another has eight children. Suppose one sibling has no children. What happens? Play with the different possibilities. Notice what is happening to the map?

Family Map

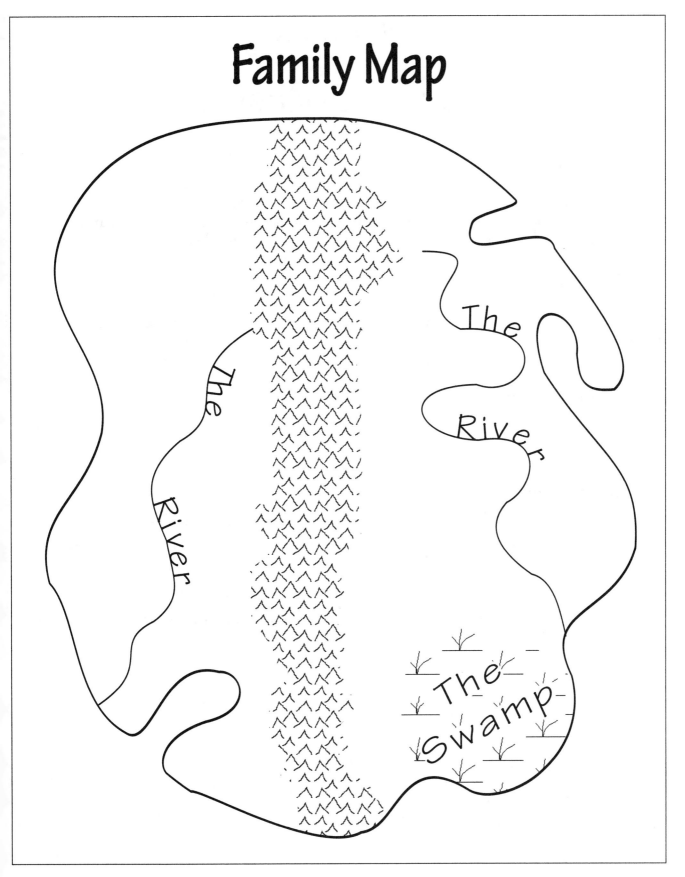

The River

The River

The Swamp

Chapter XI

Harun-al-Rashid

Other Resources:

In <u>Arabian</u> <u>Knights</u>, Harun-al-Rashid makes an appearance as the ideal Islamic caliph. You might read selections from this work at this point. The story, "Ali Baba and the Forty Thieves," is probably one of the best-known tales.

Vocabulary:

tribute	bazaars	algebra
Arabic numerals	scholar	correspondence
usurped	scimitar	dictate
ravage	sack (to sack a place)	suppress

People and Places:

Harun-Al-Rashid	Constantinople	Baghdad
Empress Irene	Nicephorus	Heraclea
Phrygia		

For Discussion:

1. Tell about the relationship between Harun-al-Rashid and Charlemagne.

2. What kind of ruler was Harun-al-Rashid? Why do you think he and Charlemagne admired each other?

3. How did Constantinople come to pay tribute to Harun-al-Rashid?

4. When did the tribute stop? Who stopped it? What was Harun-al-Rashid's response to this challenge?

Chapter **XII**

Egbert the Saxon

Other Resources:

As you focus on the Anglo-Saxon culture, you may wish to read or assign the Anglo-Saxon epic, *Beowulf*. It is typically assigned to eighth or ninth graders (and that is probably about right for independent reading). You may wish to read sections aloud to younger children. If you are including older students in your study, then a "Cliff Notes" type summary book might be helpful to you as the teacher (especially if you have blocked your own high school study of *Beowulf* out of your tortured memory). Such a tool will give you some insight into issues, literary terms, and recurrent themes/issues, typically discussed with reference to this work.

There are several editions of *Beowulf* currently in print. The Greenleaf favorite is a new verse translation by Frederick Rebsamen (HarperCollins, copyright 1991). We particularly like this translation because it attempts to recreate what English poetry was like before the French corrupted it (er, oops, "changed it"). Before William the Conqueror brought the French language to England, rhyme was not a significant element in English poetry. Alliteration, rhythm, and a characterisitc mid-line pause (ceasuran pause) were characteristic. If you're adventurous, you might try sitting around a fire one night (with the lights off or dim) and read a section out loud. This is how the poem would have been experienced when it was first written.

The Story of King Arthur

Parents need to be aware that most editions of the King Arthur stories do contain some references to magic. It is, however, one of those stories that captured the imaginations of many later authors and many later literary works build upon it in some way. If you do decide to read the Arthurian tales and legends, there are fruitful discussion possibilities in an examination of the "peaceful coexistence" between that which is Christian and that which is magical. What does this mix reveal about the culture? Does it represent a Christian World View?

Though the stories of Arthur do have a lot to do with knights and chivalry, they predate the feudal system, per se. It is more a matter of loyalty to the war-chief than full-blown feudalism. If you spend a lot of time with Arthur, you might want to spend time talking about Knights, Chivalry, and Heraldry at this point. More complete background information can be found in Chapter Thirteen, "Rollo the Viking."

Sir Gawain and the Green Knight, translated J.R.R.Tolkien. Set during Arthur's rule. We have read this aloud in our family reading times twice now, and have found it to be a real hit. The story has much to say about being true to your word EVEN when no one is watching. Can be appreciated on several levels.

Chapter XII
Egbert the Saxon
(continued)

<u>Saint Patrick's Day</u>, Joyce K. Kessel, Carolrhoda Books, 1982. Easy reader. Tells the story of the life of St. Patrick as an explanation for why his day is celebrated. A wonderful children's book (approx. 2nd-3rd grade reading level) which recounts Patrick's life as a Roman youth, his six years of slavery in Ireland, his escape to England, and then his return as a missionary to the Irish.

Vocabulary:

forefathers	devoted	clan
singular	captives	allegiance
conciliation		

People and Places:

Britons	Wales	Cornwall
Julius Caesar	Saxons	Angles
Jutes	King Arthur	Patrick
Picts	England	Egbert
Augustine (not St. Augustine of Hippo)		

For Discussion:

1. Locate England, Wales and Cornwall on the map. Locate the kingdoms of the Saxons, the Angles and the Jutes.

2. Tell about the conflict between the Britons and the Saxons. Tell how the two groups differed from one another. Tell what they had in common with each other.

3. Tell how the Gospel came to the British Isles. Who and where were the believers? Who were not Christians? What religion were they?

4. Tell how the British Christians attempted to spread the Gospel to their neighbors. How were they received? Who eventually helped them?

5. Read further about Saint Patrick. Tell how God brought great good out of the difficult circumstance of Patrick's capture and out of the enslavement of the Angle captives.

6. Tell about the life of Egbert. What kind of ruler was he? In what ways did Charlemagne influence him? Do you think Charlemagne would have been proud of him?

Chapter XIII

Rollo the Viking

Other Resources:

<u>Penguin Atlas</u>, pages 48-49 show the route of Rollo on his conquest of Normandy

<u>Viking Raiders</u>, Usborne Time Traveller Series, 1990.

<u>The Vikings</u>, Elizabeth Janeway, one of the books in Random House's "Landmark" series. Tells the story of Leif Erickson.

<u>Beorn the Proud</u>, Polland. As far as we know, this book is out of print. However, it is worth ordering a book search for it at your local used book store, or asking your local librarian to get it for you through inter-library loan, if necessary. The book tells the story of a young Irish Christian girl who is captured by Vikings during a raid on her village. She comes to live with Beorn's family and comes to realize the family's need for the Gospel. **Highly recommended!**

<u>The Black Fox of Lorne</u>, Marguerite de Angeli (author of *The Door in the Wall*).

Background Information:

The word "viking" was originally used as a verb which meant to go raiding. The Vikings were those who went raiding.

Their religion was harsh, involving human and animal sacrifice. For study of Norse mythology see <u>Bulfinch's Mythology</u> or Edith Hamilton's <u>Mythology</u>. A study of their mythology tells much about the Viking thought and culture, for only those who died in battle gained anything in the afterlife.

There were basically three groups of Norsemen (Northmen) — Norwegian, Danish, and Swedish.

The Danes and the Norwegians travelled primarily south across the North Sea. They raided along the English Channel, attacking Britain, Ireland, and parts of Europe. They did not limit themselves to targets along the sea coast, but also raided far up the channels of major rivers.

The Swedes moved across the Baltic, into Russia, down the Volga and Dnieper, and some eventually reaching as far as Baghdad! They attacked Constantinople four times, and eventually, supplied men for the Byzantine Emperor's elite Varangean guard.

Chapter XIII
Rollo the Viking
(continued)

A Few Notes on Feudalism:

The Vikings were allowed to settle in Normandy on the condition that they **swear fealty,** that is loyalty, to the French king and become his vassals. The swearing of fealty was a building block of feudalism. Therefore, a little background information on **feudalism** follows.

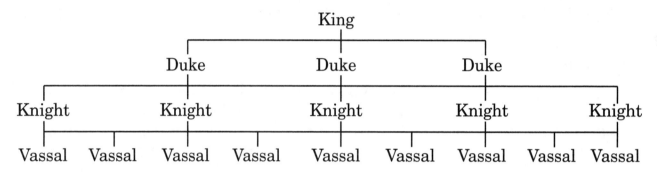

The duties of the King:

1. defend the kingdom against foreign attack
2. defend the church against internal and external enemies
3. protect the towns from attack
4. aid the helpless (orphans, widows, and the poor/needy)

The King would cede a certain area of land to his trusted men. These lords were given following duties:

1. keep order within their borders
2. hold court within their borders
3. permitted to levy the taxes of their choice on their subjects

These lords then granted to their trusted men (called vassals) a certain area of land (called fiefs) in exchange for their military and political service.

The possession of a fief was not hereditary. It could be bought back from a lord on the death of the original vassal. If a vassal was disloyal or incompetent the lord could take the fief back. The lord had the right to control the marriage of any feudal heiress. Since the vassal's son-in-law would rule the fief, the lords wanted to insure that the new vassal would be loyal. Any orphaned minor heirs of a vassal became the wards of the lord. The lord ruled the fief until the ward came of age, and because the ward performed none of the services expected of a vassal, the lord received all income from the fief until the ward came of age.

A vassal paid homage and swore fealty to his lord. He was expected to:
1. give the lord 40 days a year offensive military service
2. be on call for unlimited amount of time to defend the lord's interests militarily.
3. govern the fief
4. appear at the lord's court to advise and serve
5. pay for the knighting of the lord's oldest son
6. pay for the marriage of the lord's oldest daughter
7. pay for the ransom of a lord who was kidnapped
8. underwrite the expenses of any extraordinary expeditions. The vassals had the right to vote on whether or not to undertake such expeditions.
9. provide hospitality to the lord as required

In exchange for his service he was granted the right to:
1. mint coins
2. wage whatever private wars he wanted to undertake
3. be the final judge in local legal matters

The greater part of the nobleman's life seems to have been connected in some way with warfare. Since there was always something to fight over, the lords were always fighting or preparing to fight with somebody. If, by some chance, there came a time of peace, the nobility honed their skills through participation in tournaments. Most of what we associate with the Middle Ages (knighthood, castles and the code of chivalry, i.e. the rules of behavior the noble knight was expected to follow) grew out of this penchant for warfare. See A Tournament of Knights, by Joe Lasker (Harper Trophy, 1986).

A **KNIGHT** was a professional mounted warrior who came from the upper class. He went through an extended period of training and apprenticeship that required him to serve first as a page and then as a squire before he could be knighted. Originally only military virtues were required of the knight, but eventually qualities of courtesy were expected. These qualities of courtesy are specifically included within a code of conduct that is referred to as "The Code of Chivalry." According to this code, a knight was expected to demonstrate a devotion to fair play and a willingness to defend the weak and helpless. He was also expected to show his devotion to the Church and respect for all women.

The Church attempted to temper the conflict as much as possible. Through its efforts women, children and clergy were declared to be immune from attack. As you read the lives of the rest of these "Famous Men..." you might ask how well they lived up to The Code of Chivalry.

HERALDRY was a means of identifying knights. As a knight's face and build were hidden under armor, it was generally impossible to identify a knight unless you knew his heraldry (the design on his shield). The design might often tell a lot about the individual's family history. It might also depict those things most valued by the knight. (See Design Your Own Coat of Arms, Dover Press.)

Because no one knew when their own region would be attacked, those who could afford to make their homes into castles, did so. (And only the Lord's could afford to do so.) We often tend to confuse castles with palaces. Any study of castles will quickly end that. Initially, they were made of wood, usually built on a high spot, surrounded by wide ditches or walls. Later they became the structures we think of them as — stone buildings with draw bridges and moats. The English style castles that we usually picture were largely

Chapter XIII
Rollo the Viking
(continued)

built under Edward III, and so David Macauley's book, <u>Castle</u>, is suggested as a reading to accompany chapter XXVIII which is about Edward III's son, Edward the Black Prince.

While the Church was able to temper some of the warfare, it also participated in the feudal system. Churchmen were often vassals. This meant that Church offices were often controlled by lay Lords. Kings appointed priests and bishops. This led to a division of loyalties (church or state?) and Church's increasing role as a player in political system (with all the concern for political expediency that goes with it).

There were three main classes of people in feudal society:

1. The **CLERGY** were expected to concern themselves with spiritual matters. They were the priests, monks, teachers, historians, copiers and preservers of books. They operated hospitals and schools and offered shelter to travellers.

2. The **NOBILITY** were expected to rule and to fight. During their leisure time they would hunt (either with bows and arrows, hounds or hawks), play games, drink, and listen to minstrels. The women ran the household and looked after the children. For the most part, the nobility were neither especially well educated nor refined. Nobody used forks. (Take THAT, Miss Manners!)

3. The **PEASANTS** lived harsh and simple lives. Their dwellings were made out of whatever they could find — wood, mud or some combination of the above. Their diet was simple — brown bread, beer or wine, and the vegetables they grew in their gardens. Meat was a special treat. On Holy Days they feasted and partied.

A Note on the Church:

The Church during the Middle Ages became more and more political as time went on. Although Charlemagne considered the Pope to be a spiritual, not a political authority, he muddied the waters somewhat when he allowed the **Pope** to crown him emperor. Later popes cited Charlemagne's coronation as precedent for the right of the Church to select and consecrate kings and other secular rulers. Charlemagne himself used his status as protector of the Pope to take on many duties that had previously been responsibilities of the church alone. He "appointed Church prelates, summoned Church councils, instituted ecclesiastical reforms and disposed of Church lands." (<u>Outline of Medieval History</u>, McGarry and Wahl, page 124.) While Charlemagne may have used his power well, the precedent was set and those who followed him were often motivated solely by the desire to increase their own political power.

In the 9th century the Church became more and more a secular power. With the rise of feudalism (during the 10th and 11th centuries) the Church and the State had many overlapping jurisdictions. Spiritual concerns were diminished, and Church appointments were often used as a way to reward political allies. Because highly placed Church officials participated in the election of the popes, those who received their appointments because they had performed political service would look to the one who had appointed them, rather than to the spiritual qualifications of a papal candidate.

Even so, the Papacy managed to remain largely independent and uncorrupted through the 12th century.

Organizing the Lesson:

1. Decide how much you want to cover about Knights and Chivalry at this point. A lot of the heraldry, castle building activities could be saved for a later chapter — for instance, the chapter on "Henry II and His Sons." Remember the period covered in this chapter is 802-837 A.D. The Vikings will continue to cause trouble for about another two hundred years. As you begin to study the "high kings" of England, there will be opportunity to spend more times with the topics related to Chivalry.

2. Your students have some background in the Norse mindset from reading the first few chapters in <u>Famous Men of the Middle Ages</u>. You might take a little time out now and concentrate on the Vikings, themselves.

3. Read <u>Time Traveller's Guide to Viking Raiders</u>, Usborne, for an overview of Viking life and customs. You might want to construct the <u>Make This Viking Settlement</u> paper cut-out model produced by Usborne.

4. Read Elizabeth Janeway's <u>The Vikings</u> (Landmark Series by Random House). This book tells the story of Leif Erickson. Check your library for other books on Leif or his dad Erik the Red. There may be lots of out-of-print choices available there or at your local used book store. You could also read <u>Beorn the Proud</u> or <u>The Black Fox of Lorne</u> out loud or assign it to be read independently. It makes a good family read-aloud.

5. Read "Rollo the Viking," <u>Famous Men of the Middle Ages</u>.

Vocabulary:

pirates	cathedral	dismayed	generous	fortify
besiegers	encamped	scarce	feuds	
vassals	persuasion	serfs	duchy	

People and Places:

Norsemen	Northmen	Labrador	Leif the Lucky
Vinland	Europe	Rollo the Walker	Seine
Paris	Newfoundland	Norway	Rouen
Normandy	Feudal System		

For Discussion:

1. Who were the Vikings? What did they value? What did they believe about God?

2. Tell about Rollo. Why was he called "the Walker?"

3. What did the bishop advise the people of Rouen to do? Did it turn out to be good advice? Explain. Tell about the rest of Rollo's campaign.

4. Tell about Rollo's encounter with Charles the Simple. Under what conditions was Rollo allowed to settle in Normandy? What kind of ruler did Rollo prove to be? Be specific.

5. Tell about the basic structure of the feudal system.

Chapter XIV

Alfred the Great

Other Resources:

Penguin Atlas, pages 46-47 show the division of England between Alfred and the Danes.

Vocabulary:

piracy	parchment	ballad
amusements	ravage	vexation
minstrel		

People and Places:

Alfred	Ethelwulf	West Saxons
Guthram		

For Discussion:

1. Once again, look at the maps in the Cultural Atlas of the Middle Ages to see where the different groups of Vikings settled or travelled.

2. Tell about Alfred's childhood. What kind of person was he?

3. Tell about Alfred's battle with the invading Danes.

4. Both Alfred and Clovis are considered by historians to be Christian kings. That is, each man made some profession of faith in Jesus. How would you compare the lives of the two men? Which man would you have rather served? Tell why and support your answer with specific examples.

Chapter XV

Henry the Fowler

Other Resources:

Penguin Atlas, pages 48-49 show the area conquered by the Magyar invaders and the area ruled by Henry as the Kingdom of Germany

Vocabulary:

sole	mere	fowler
falcon	falconry	rout/routed
truce	invincible	fortified
Otto	assumed (as in *assumed the title*)	

People and Places:

Magyars	Conrad	Franconia
Hartz Mountains	Saxony	Aix-la-Chapelle
Hungary	Holy Roman Empire	

For Discussion:

1. Falconry was also called the "Sport of Kings." What is falconry? What did it involve? Do you know how they train the birds? Consider assigning a little research project to your student(s) about falconry.

2. What was the Holy Roman Empire? What area did it cover? What did the Holy Roman Empire have to do with Charlemagne?

Chapter XVI

Canute the Great

Other Resources

Penguin Atlas, pages 58-59 show the extent of the territory ruled by Canute (the Danish Empires)

Vocabulary:

slight   treachery   feeble
prosperous

People and Places:

Denmark/Danes   Anglo-Saxons   Ethelred
Normandy   Sweyn   Canute
Edmund Ironside

For Discussion:

1. Briefly describe the rulers of England after the time of Alfred the Great. Who invaded? Who did they attack? Where did they come from? Who won and who fled?

2. The text says that Canute ruled wisely. Do you agree with that or not? Give specific examples to support your answer.

3. What is flattery? Read Psalm 5:9 and Proverbs 29:5. How did Canute respond to flattery?

4. The incident in which Canute commands the waves to turn back is well-known. Consider having your student's act it out or put together a radio play complete with sound effects.

Chapter XVII

El Cid

Other Resources:

Penguin Atlas, pages 62-63 show the territory of Leon & Castile at the time of El Cid

Vocabulary:

mire	leper	garments
vision	vanquished	banished
fortified	besieged	irrigated
citadel	sally	routed
mosque	embalm	

People and Places:

Rodrigo Diaz de Bivar	Saracens	Castile
Leon	Aragon	Fernando of Castile
Moors	Alcocer	Valencia
Toledo	the river Guadalquivir	

For Discussion:

1. Use the map of Spain found on pages 72-73 of the Cultural Atlas of the Middle Ages to find the place names mentioned in the chapter.

2. Which parts of the story are legendary and which are more historical? Why do you answer as you do?

3. How would you describe El Cid? What did he spend most of his life doing? How successful would you say he was in life?

4. Describe how he defeated the Saracens after his death.

Chapter XVIII

Edward the Confessor

Other Resources:

William Shakespeare, <u>MacBeth</u>. (Check out the "Cliff Notes" Complete Study Edition).

Vocabulary:

pirate   usurper   ancient

People and Places:

Normandy   Kent   Essex
Norwegians/Norway   Kerdric   Macbeth
Duncan   Malcolm   Scotland
Westminster Abbey

For Discussion:

1. Describe the difference between the Danish kings that followed Canute and Canute, himself. Who followed them? What were they like?

2. Why was Edward called *the Confessor*? What kind of king was he? How did the English people feel about him?

3. How did Normandy come to play such an influential role in England's history?

4. Tell the story of the Scottish nobleman Macbeth. You might read the story in Charles Lamb's Tales from Shakespeare. Better yet, read the play together or listen to a taped recording of a performance of the play. Check your local library (or inter-library loan) for a copy of a tape. Check with local community theaters about live performances of the play. You might also see if area college drama students or members of a community theater group would be willing to prepare and perform a scene or two for your group.

Chapter **XIX**

William the Conqueror

Other Resources:

Penguin Atlas, pages 60-61 show the territories of Normandy and England ruled by William

National Geographic, August 1966. Contains pictures of the complete Tapestry. Look in thrift stores, Goodwill stores, and used books stores. If you had two copies you could cut the tapestry out and put it together, making your own miniature Bayeux Tapestry. It really does tell the entire story of the invasion, and is impressive when you can see it all in one piece. I almost hesitate to even make this suggestion, because it is not a really easy magazine to find, but if you are able to pull it off, it is well worth the effort.

Vocabulary:

enforce a claim	embassy	stockade
extensive	curfew	

People and Places:

William, Duke of Normandy	Normandy	Rouen
Harold Godwinson	Hastings/Senlac	Domesday Book
Mantes	Scotland	

For Discussion:

1. Why did William invade England? What was the basis of his claim to the throne?

2. Tell about the Battle of Hastings. How were the English forces handicapped?

3. Before William's invasion, England was peopled by three main groups of people, the Angles, the Saxons and the Celts. William brought a new group — the Normans. With his rule, the Normans were, as you might expect, the new powerful class. When you read the Robin Hood legends later in your study, you will notice the tension between Norman and Anglo-Saxon England. This is why. There were other changes brought by William: 1. The introduction of the French language (the influence of French language) to the English. 2. The introduction of a formal feudal system replaced local autonomy in many places, and, at the national level, strengthened the resources that the King could call on in an emergency.

4. What was the Domesday Book, and what was its purpose?

Chapter XIX
William the Conqueror
(continued)

5. Create your own Domesday Book. One child might be designated, "Official Assessor," while another may record all that that child reports to him. Or you might assign each child to record all his or her own belongings. Talk about how you would go about doing that for a large group of people.

6. You might have your students copy (draw) panels from the Tapestry. Make it as simple OR as elaborate as you wish. You could draw one panel only to each sheet of paper and then link them all together for display OR you could draw a section onto a sheet of white cloth and have your student fill in with some simple embroidery stitches and complete a section that way. (Or go ahead, impress the neighbors — Do the **WHOLE** thing!)

Chapter XX

Pope Gregory VII and Emperor Henry IV

Other Resources:

Penguin Atlas, pages 62-63 show the territory ruled by Henry IV as Holy Roman Emporer (labeled "German Empires")

Vocabulary:

magistrates	merge	royal insignia	fend (for themselves)
pondered	convene/convened	excommunicating	deposing
preside	beseech	successive	cease
apostolic	restore	imperial	siege
exile	iniquity	coarse	attire

People and Places:

Hildebrand	Pope Gregory	Henry IV
Germany	Alps	Canossa

Discussion:

1. How were Church leaders chosen? What problems might there be under this system?

2. Who was Hildebrand? What was he like? What does his choice of Gregory for his papal name tell you about him?

3. Who was Henry IV? How would you describe his character?

4. Tell about the conflict between Henry IV and Gregory? What is significant about Canossa?

5. Do you think Henry's repentance was sincere? Explain your answer. How can you tell the difference between repentance and regret over the consequences of a person's actions? How did Henry behave after Canossa?

6. Tell about Gregory's death. What were his final words? Can you think of specific scriptures that would apply to his last statement? Tell how they apply (the world does not hate you... any of the lives of the prophets).

Chapter **XXI**

Peter the Hermit

Other Resources:

Penguin Atlas, pages 64-65 show the route of the First Crusade

Vocabulary:

pilgrims	pilgrimages	caliph
sepulchre	portion	

People and Places:

Holy Land	Turks	Clermont, France
Pope Urban II	Holy Sepulchre	Italy
Crusade	Hungary	
Champions of the Cross		

Discussion:

1. Why did Christians make pilgrimages?

2. When the Turks took over the Holy Land, what changes came about?

3. Tell how the First Crusade began. Who went? What was their purpose? What provisions did they take with them? How did they conduct themselves along the way?

4. Trace their route on a map.

5. After Peter the Hermit left the first group, who did he join up with?

6. Tell about Godfrey's army. Continue to trace Godfrey's route on a map. What cities did he have to conquer in order to reach Jerusalem? Describe those battles.

7. After Jerusalem was taken, what happened to Peter and Godfrey?

8. Many who are not Christians point to the Crusades as an example of typical Christian behavior. Many will say that they are not Christians themselves, because they see the Crusaders as typical of all Christians. How would you answer this charge? (This would make a good essay assignment.)

Chapter **XXII**

Frederick Barbarossa

Other Resources

Penguin Atlas, pages 68-69 show the territory ruled by Frederick. The text on page 70 gives a brief synopsis of the route and accomplishments of Frederick on the Third Crusade.

Vocabulary:

majestic	fortifications	subdue
league	defy/defied	implored
treason	summon	misconduct
Christendom	peasants	slumber
ancient		

People and Places:

Frederick Barbarossa	Lombardy	Milan
Henry the Lion	Saxony	Bavaria
Saladin	Palestine	Antioch

Discussion:

1. What was Frederick's quarrel with the Lombards? What was the outcome of the dispute?

2. What did Frederick devote himself to accomplishing within Germany?

3. After the death of Frederick, the quarrelling of the nobles continued. Otto of the Silver Hand by Howard Pyle, is set in the time of Emperor Fredrick, grandson of Barbarossa. Although set in a later period, the picture Pyle paints of life amid warring robber-barons, makes this a good book to read at this point.

4. Tell about the death of Barbarossa. How did the German people feel about him? Why do you think they felt the way they did?

Chapter XXIII

Henry II and His Sons

Other Resources:

<u>Penguin Atlas</u>, pages 68-69 and 70-71 show the territory ruled by Henry and then lost by his sons to Philip Augustus of France

For Older Readers: <u>Murder in the Cathedral</u>, T.S. Eliot, a verse play about the death of Thomas Becket, Archbishop of Canterbury

Becket, (the movie, now on video) stars Richard Burton and Peter O'Toole, the contrast between Becket's wild (i.e. wine, women, and carousing) early life and his more serious life as a churchman is emphasized.

<u>The Lion in Winter</u> (the movie, now on video) starring Katherine Hepburn and Peter O'Toole looks at the aging King Henry and his very dysfunctional family. King Henry has had his wife, Eleanor, imprisoned in one of his castles for plotting against him. However, since it is Christmas, he summons her for a family gathering with their sons. The portrayal of the sons' (lack of) character is apparently fairly accurate. See this movie if you think you'd like to live in a castle. December in Northern France without central heat was not much fun. Note the scene where the king has to break through the ice in his wash-bucket in order to splash his face first thing in the morning. There is too much talk and too little action to make it attractive to elementary aged kids (even without other considera-tions that follow, but Rob declares adamantly that it is one of his all-time favorite movies, while Cyndy has trouble staying awake and marvels at his lack of taste.

CAUTION TO PARENTS: Much of this movie could be a useful supplement to study of the period, and I am including this description in the guide **in case** you are considering renting it for just that purpose. However, during one scene Philip of France confronts Henry's boys about an earlier relationship he has had with one of them. The description is none too discrete and involves homosexuality. It could be fast forwarded, but screen it yourself first before you decide to show it. The allegation, by the way, has some basis in historical fact.

Vocabulary:

sprig	broom plant	domain
turbulent	brutal	martyr
pious	canonized	venerate
conspiracy	penance	scourges

People and Places:

Geoffrey Plantagenet   Anjou, France   Matilda
Thomas Becket   Canterbury Cathedral   Eleanor of Aquitane
Richard the Lion-Hearted   Henry II

Discussion:

1. Describe the relationship between Henry and Thomas Becket. Why do you think Henry made Thomas Archbishop? What does the choice show about Henry's attitude toward the church? What was he hoping to accomplish by putting Becket in charge of the clergy?

2. Was Henry pleased with his choice? Explain your answer.

3. Describe the death of Thomas Becket. What was Henry's response? If Henry were tried for the murder and you were a juror, how would you vote? Guilty or not guilty? Explain your answer.

4. Who were Henry's sons. Describe each of them.

5. What was their relationship with their father? What type of father do you think he was? Why do you answer the way you do?

6. How did the sons feel about each other? Give specific examples.

This is the period most associated with all the things children (and some of the rest of us even) love about the Middle Ages: knights, castles, lords and ladies, and so on and so on. And this is a good point to take a little time and revel in the fun of the period.

And to that end, a few suggestions:

1. Teach the story of Richard the Lion-hearted — historically. Point out his strengths <u>and</u> his failings. Contrast outward appearances: strength, brave deeds, attractive appearance with inward character.

2. Discuss the ways in which the outward appearances helped build the image of Richard that comes down to us in the legends and stories we love to hear. Then, if you like, read <u>The Story of Robin Hood</u>. As you read, keep the questions of historical accuracy lightly in view. Don't kill the fun of the story, but gently help your students to analyze as they "play."

3. This is also a good time to look at daily life in the middle ages. What was it like to live in the town, in the village, on the manor? Look at social structures. Look at chivalry — knights and castles. Have a medieval feast, if you are so inclined.

Chapter XXIII
Henry the Second and His Sons
(continued)

4. You may be aware of a Medieval Festival in your area. Sometimes demonstrations of medieval activities are held, usually put on by the Society for Creative Anachronisms. These can be an excellent way to put yourselves in the period and really experience life in this time period. The festivals can be an excellent resource. However, our experience has been that the Creative Anachronism groups vary greatly from place to place and group to group. Some are purely fun, others have members who are more involved in the "Dungeons and Dragons" type activities and some groups are more interested in magical themes. The key is to always "test the spirits." I John 4:1.

5. Although the literature of this period is full of the fantastic — dragons and such, and although we do think it's possible to work with much of it while still maintaining a Christian perspective (i.e. much is allegorical, much symbolic, much just plain "pretend,") it is a period that is often adopted as a background for role-playing games like Dungeons and Dragons. We do **NOT** recommend making this a part of your study. D & D materials draw from some occultic sources and encourage a fascination with the occult that we would **STRONGLY** advise parents to avoid. Although some might feel that the use of role-playing games like Dungeons & Dragons would add to one's appreciation of the Medieval world, we do **NOT**.

"Richard the Lion-Hearted"

Vocabulary:

valor	conferred	accolade	besiegers
heralds	vied	valiant	astounded
intercede/interceded	pout	tyrannical	

People and Places:

Leopold of Austria	Blondel	Runnymeade	Magna Carta

Discussion:

1. Describe Richard's reputation with the English people. Does it seem to have been accurate? How and how not? (recall the phrase, "absence makes the heart grow fonder...")

2. How much time did Richard spend in England? Where was he most of the time?

3. Describe Richard's role in the Crusades.

4. Tell about his return trip. How was it interrupted?

5. How was the news of Richard's capture received at home? How was the news of his release received? What does John's response tell you about his character?

Other resources:

The Story of Robin Hood, Howard Pyle

The Story of Robin Hood, Sidney Lanier

Robin Hood, (the movie, now on video) starring Errol Flynn. A classic retelling of the tale.

We do **NOT** recommend the more recent remake, *Robin Hood: Prince of Thieves*. Too much occult weirdness (not in any of the original) and a hopelessly anachronistic Kevin Costner.

When Knights Were Bold, out of print, but check your libraries. Interlibrary loan requests sometimes turn up books that your librarian has never seen.

Living in Castle Times, Usborne (early elementary)

Knights and Castles, Usborne (middle elementary)

Medieval Feast, Aliki, all the preparations that the Lord's household went through to get ready for a BIG party.

The Minstrel in the Tower (grades 2-4) is also set in this time period

Usborne makes a very nice medieval "Make this Model..." series. You might want to put a model town or village together. They also make a castle and cathedral. We'll deal more with those topics soon so you may want to wait. (A nifty feature is that all four can be fit together to make one large set, for those who are so inclined — and blessed with a place to put it when it's all done!)

"John Lackland"

Other resources:

The Magna Charta, James Daugherty, now back in print, has a good section on daily life in medieval England, the stories of John and Richard as well as a description of other documents (Mayflower Compact, Declaration of Independence) that are in something of the same tradition as the Magna Carta. To give you just a taste, here is a section that describes John's behavior on his first trip to Ireland after his father crowned him King of Ireland:

"Shortly after their landing, a delegation of shaggy Irish chieftains came to pay homage to their new overlord. John and his knights were very amused at the wild appearance of his barbaric subjects and laughed heartily in their faces. When the chieftains knelt to swear allegiance the new overlord could not resist pulling and tweaking their long curly beards and laughing even louder. This is never a safe thing to do to an Irishman."

Chapter XXIII
Henry the Second and His Sons
(continued)

Note: Lackland was a nickname given to John by his father at his birth. Having given most of his land to his older sons, he had little left to give his new son. Thus he called him John Lack-land. The name proved appropriate for his later life as well, as John managed to lose all the family's possessions in France. And when he signed the Magna Carta, he lost many of his absolute rights in England as well.

While the Robin Hood legend flatters Richard unfairly, it does paint a pretty reasonable picture of Prince John. I guess, compared to John, Richard did look pretty good to the English people.

Vocabulary:

tyrannical   oppose

People and Places:

Runnymede   Magna Carta (alternate spelling: Charta)

Discussion:

1. Describe John Lackland. How would you compare him with Richard?

2. How did John and Richard get along?

3. How did John lose Normandy?

4. What was significant about the Magna Carta? What did the document contain?

5. Since John died, no other English King has ever been named John. Why do you think this is so?

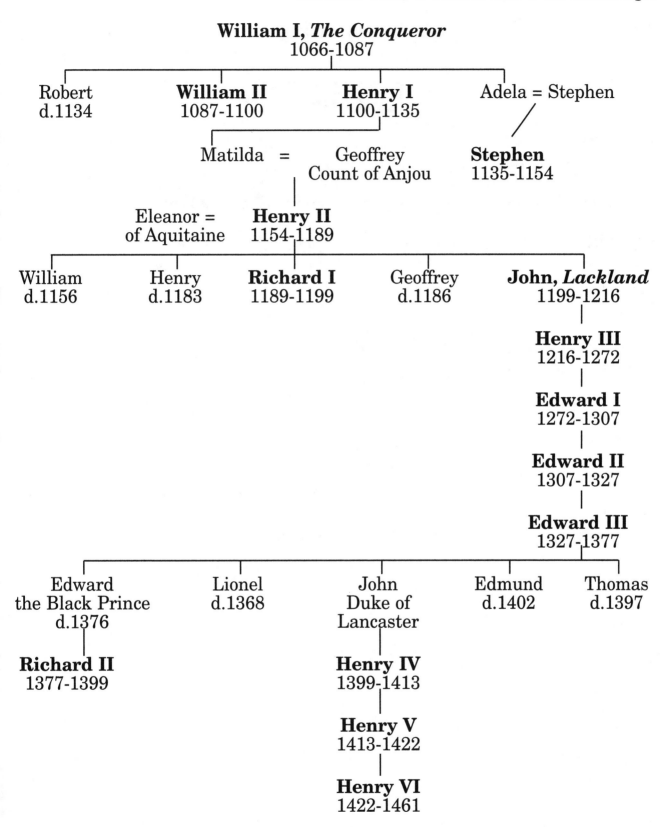

William I, *The Conqueror*
1066-1087

Robert
d.1134

William II
1087-1100

Henry I
1100-1135

Adela = Stephen

Matilda = Geoffrey
Count of Anjou

Stephen
1135-1154

Eleanor =
of Aquitaine

Henry II
1154-1189

William
d.1156

Henry
d.1183

Richard I
1189-1199

Geoffrey
d.1186

John, *Lackland*
1199-1216

Henry III
1216-1272

Edward I
1272-1307

Edward II
1307-1327

Edward III
1327-1377

Edward
the Black Prince
d.1376

Lionel
d.1368

John
Duke of
Lancaster

Edmund
d.1402

Thomas
d.1397

Richard II
1377-1399

Henry IV
1399-1413

Henry V
1413-1422

Henry VI
1422-1461

Chapter XXIV

Louis IX

Other Resources

Penguin Atlas, pages 78-79 show Europe during the reign of Louis IX

Vocabulary:

allegiance	fervently	obliged
regent	expedition	hindrance
chivalrous		

People and Places:

Mediterranean	Children's Crusade	Damietta
Cairo	Sorbonne	Tunis
Pope Boniface		

Discussion:

1. What was the "Children's Crusade?"

2. Why did Louis leave on his Crusade? Where did he want to go? Why? How well did Louis do?

3. For what do the French people remember Louis?

Chapter **XXV**

St. Francis and St. Dominic

Vocabulary:

degenerate	high purposes	bureaucracies	reform
prosperous	indulged	dejected	renounce
devote	resolved	repent	acquire
encounter	opposition	itinerant	evicted
acquisition	basilica	devise	administrator
auspices	inquisition	reputation	stringent means
recant	drastic	contaminate	excesses

People and Places:

Francis	Franciscans	Dominic
Dominicans	Simon de Montfort	

Discussion:

1. Describe Francis' family's background.

2. How did Francis change his thinking? His lifestyle?

3. How were the Franciscans different from other monastic movements? What was the primary focus of the Franciscans?

4. How were the Franciscans received by the Church officials? Why do you think the Church officials responded the way they did? Describe the Pope's response to them. Can you think of reasons why the Pope would give his support to the Franciscans? (Hint: some may be less than altruistic.)

5. What did Dominic find to be lacking in the lives of the clergy and the lay people? How did he plan to fix the problem? What were (and are) the Dominicans known for?

6. Describe the relationship between Simon de Montfort and Dominic.

7. In what ways may the Dominicans have influenced the history of England (and even the United States)?

8. After the deaths of their founders, what happened to the Franciscans and the Dominicans? Do you think Francis and Dominic would have been pleased? Explain your answer.

Chapter XXVI

Robert Bruce

Other Resources:

Adam of the Road, by Elizabeth Janet Gray, illustrated by Robert Lawson, 1942 Newberry Medal Winner. Set in the time of Edward I (1292, to be exact) who reigned from 1272-1307. Eleven-year-old Adam suddenly discovers his father, a wandering minstrel, has disappeared and his dog, Nick, has been stolen, so he sets off to track them and find them, traveling to fairs in several cities.

Door in the Wall, by Marguerite de Angeli, 1949 Newberry Medal Winner. Set in the reign of Edward III. The main character's father is away with the king, fighting the Scottish wars.

Castle, by David Macaulay. Describes the building of castles under King Edward I. Other castle books you might enjoy: Life in Castle Times, (Usborne), The Truth About Castles.

Vocabulary:

vassal   cleft

People and Places:

Baliol	Stone of Scone	Sir William Wallace	Bannockburn
Edward I	Edward II	Edward III	

Discussion:

1. Describe the way in which Scotland became a part of England.

2. Why did the Scots rebel against Edward? How successful was their rebellion? Describe what happened.

3. Who was Robert Bruce? What was his part in the conflict between England and Scotland? Which side would have referred to the conflict as a rebellion? Which side would have called it a battle for independence? What are the differences in meaning?

4. Tell the story of Robert Bruce and the spider. What lesson did Robert learn? How did he apply it?

5. Between the years 1300 and 1350 approximately, the Black Plague decimated Europe's population. Have your students research the topic. (The plague plays a major part in the story told in Door in the Wall.) How often did the plagues recur? Why did they start or stop? When did they finally end? What reasons are given for that? What was life like during a plague? How did people generally behave? Were there any notable exceptions?

Chapter **XXVII**

Marco Polo

Other Resources::

"Marco Polo," <u>Usborne Book of Explorers</u>, pages 16-17. Includes nice map of the Polo family's journey.

Vocabulary:

envoy	gorgeous	crimson
satin	damask	velvet

People and Places:

Kublai Khan	Cathay	Peking/Beijing
Venice	Persia	Black Sea
Tatar	Genoa	Venice

Discussion:

1. Describe Marco Polo's journey. What was its purpose? Did they accomplish what they set out to accomplish?

2. For further reading you might read aloud from <u>The Travels of Marco Polo</u>, or check your library or used book dealer for <u>Marco Polo</u> (Landmark World History series).

3. Assuming that reliable mail service operated between China and Venice (I guess not all that much has changed, after all...), pretend you are Marco Polo and write a letter home to Mom describing your adventures. If the very thought of reliable mail service stretches the imagination too painfully, write an entry for your journal instead.

Chapter XXVIII

Edward the Black Prince

Vocabulary:

bar the claim	forfeit	hard pressed
unhorsed	win his spurs	onset

People and Places:

Edward the Black Prince	Philip of Valois	Salic Law
Crecy	Calais	Poitiers

Discussion:

1. Explain how the King of England was both king of England **and** vassal of the King of France. Why should this present a problem? What would have to happen in order for the relationship to change?

2. On what did Edward base **his** claim to the French crown? Why did the French king reject Edward's claim? Describe King Edward's response to the rejection of his claim.

3. Who was the Black Prince and how did he come by that name?

4. Tell about the Black Prince and the Battle of Crecy.

5. Tell about the Battle of Poitiers. What was its outcome?

6. Why do we call Edward the "Black Prince," instead of Edward IV?

A Note on the Genealogical Chart, *The Succession in France in 1328 and 1422*:

The three sons of Philip IV each became king of France in turn, but each died without leaving a male heir. Philip IV's fourth child, Isabella, had married King Edward II of England. When Charles IV, the last son of Philip IV, died in 1328, the French crown passed to his first cousin, Philip VI of Valois. Edward III who assumed the English crown in the same year was then asked to do homage to the new French king for the provinces which his family ruled in France (primarily Gascony and Aquitaine). Edward objected, and pointed out that he was the eldest male grandchild of Philip IV and therefore had a better claim to the French throne than did Philip of Valois, who was Philip IV's nephew. Thus began the 100 Years War. In 1415, Henry V revived his great-grandfather's claim to the throne and by force of arms, forced Charles VI to declare that *his* great-grandfather's claim had been inferior to Henry's great-grandfather's. Henry V thought he had settled the entire matter by marrying Charles VI's daughter and having himself and his son declared the heirs to the French crown. When Henry V and Charles VI both died in 1422, Henry VI did succeed to both crowns, briefly. But the French nobility eventually rallied around Charles VII and partially inspired by a French peasant girl (Joan of Arc) managed to expel the English forces and return the French crown to the House of Valois.

The Succession in France in 1328 and 1422

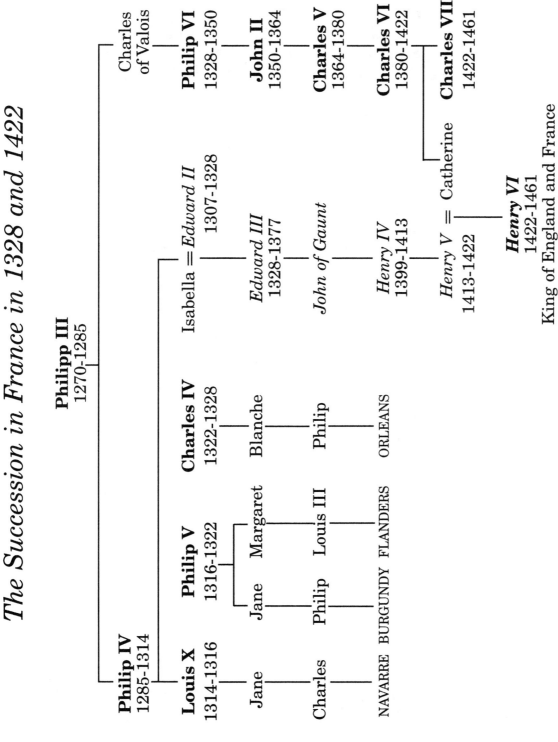

Chapter XXIX

William Tell and Arnold Von Winkelried

Vocabulary:

canton

People and Places:

William Tell	Gessler	Austria
Lake Lucerne	The Forest Cantons	The Republic of Switzerland
Winkelried		

Discussion:

1. Look at a physical map of Switzerland. Describe the land. Why do you think the Forest Cantons were left alone for such a long time?

2. Tell the story of William Tell. (Good choice for a play — radio or otherwise. If real props are used, make sure your "William" doesn't have a bone to pick with your "William Tell, Jr.")

3. Listen to the William Tell Overture by Rossini. Do you think the music fits the action of the story? The mood of the story? Explain your answer.

6. Tell the story of Arnold Von Winkelried.

Chapter **XXX**

Tamerlane

Other Resources

<u>Penguin Atlas</u>, pages 94-95 show the territory conquered by Tamerlane

Vocabulary:

devastate	taunt	humiliate
indulged	disband	

People and Places:

Timour the Lame	Genghis Kahn	Turkistan
India	Russia	Bajazet

Discussion:

1. Show Tamerlane's homelands on a map.

2. What was Tamerlane's goal in life? On what did he base his desires? What do you think about this goal of his? What goals do you have for your life? (This smells like a good essay topic, but insist that your students really think about their answer before they actually start to write something that looks like a near final draft. In some cases it will be easier and also more pleasant for your student to think through this and discuss it more informally. The goal is for them to interact with their study, and think about what they are studying. Don't feel like this HAS to be an essay assignment.)

3. Describe Tamerlane. If the election for "RULER OF THE WORLD!" were held today, would Tamerlane get your vote? Why or why not?

Chapter XXXI

Henry V

Other Resources:

Penguin Atlas, pages 96-97 show the combined Kingdom of England and France conquered and ruled by Henry V

The Canterbury Tales, Geoffrey Chaucer, Written between 1386 and 1400. This work is usually studied as a part of English Literature in senior high. If you have a high schooler studying with you, now would be a good time to assign this to them. As I suggested with Beowulf, you may want to buy some sort of guide book that will give you some idea of issues, themes, poetic background that would be emphasized with regard to a study of this work. At least assign the "Prologue." Chaucer gives an excellent sketch of Medieval life in these tales. But before you assign any other tales, be sure to read the section yourself. You might remember from your own High School English Class that some sections are "bawdier than others." Some sections you will want to skip altogether. For younger students, you might read selections from "The Prologue," where Chaucer describes each of the pilgrims — who they are, what they do, why they are going on this pilgrimage, etc.

Chanticleer and the Fox, illus by Barbara Cooney is a Caldecott Medal winner that you might want to read to your younger children. It retells one of the stories from Chaucer.

There is a new children's illustrated Canterbury Tales which retells three of Chaucer's stories. It is illustrated by Trina Schart Hyman (who did the wonderful illustrations for St.George and the Dragon, the 1984 Caldecott Award winner).

Cliff Notes, Complete Study Edition, "The Prologue" also Cliff Notes, Complete Study Edition, "The Wife of Bath's Tale."

Also: You might read, listen to, or watch Shakespeare's Henry V.

Vocabulary:

good grace	buckram	vicious	merriment
garrison	trenches	feeble	regent

People and Places:

Prince Hal/Henry V	John Falstaff	Normandy
Agincourt	Rouen	

Discussion:

1. What was Henry like as a youth? Tell about his relationship with Sir John Falstaff. When did the relationship change? How did it change?

2. Why did Henry go to war against France? What did he hope to accomplish? How successful was he?

3. Why do you think Henry refused to let the poor people of Rouen pass through his lines? Apply Romans 12:20 to situation. [Ed. Note: We obviously don't think much of Henry's tactics here...]

4. Describe Henry's treatment of the French king. What did the treaty stipulate? How was it carried out?

Chapter XXXII

Joan of Arc

Other Resources:

Joan of Arc, by Dianne Stanley: This is her newest book and the illustrations are exquisite. Stanley's style uses bright colors, intricate borders, and an almost unbelievable attention to fine detail, but this is not just a picture book. The text tells the complex story of Joan in a straightforward, complete fashion. There is much more information here than you will get in any textbook, and compares favorably with many adult biographies of Joan.

Vocabulary:

peasant	brooded	fancy
jubilant	coronation	sorcery
stake		

People and Places:

Domremy	Charles VII of France	Duke of Burgundy

For Discussion:

1. Tell the story of Joan of Arc. What did she do and why did she do it?

2. In evaluating the story (and life) of Joan of Arc, there are essentially three possibilities. Either Joan was lying, Joan was deluded, or Joan was telling the truth. Discuss each possibility. What do you conclude? If you are unable to reach a single conclusion — explain why.

Chapter **XXXIII**

Gutenberg

Other Resources:

Fine Print, by Joann Johansen Burch. Tells about the life of Gutenberg as well as providing some clear technical information about block printing.

Ink on His Fingers, Louise Vernon. Biographical fiction. Tells about the life and work of Gutenberg as seen through the eyes of his young apprentice. Independent reading level: upper elementary. Good read-aloud.

Vocabulary:

tinkerer   block printing   contrive
wizard

People and Places:

Strasburg   Fust   Lorenz Coster
Harlem   the Netherlands   Aldus Manutius
Venice

Discussion:

1. How were books made when Gutenberg was a boy? How were block books an improvement? What were some of the problems or difficulties associated with block printing?

2. Tell about Gutenberg's work. What problems did he have with the wood type? Why did he switch to metal type?

3. As you have studied, you have read about many people who struggled against incredible odds or against intense opposition in order to reach some goal or vision. What are some of the reasons behind their perseverence? What do you think helped them to keep going? What lessons can you learn from their lives? Applications? Activity: Block Printing

Chapter **XXXIV**

Warwick the Kingmaker

Other Resources:

William Shakespeare, <u>Richard II</u>.

Vocabulary:

wardens	sentry	misrule
reform	petition	insane
victors		

People and Places:

the Earl of Warwick	Lancastrians	Yorkists
War of the Roses		

Discussion:

1. I had some trouble keeping everything straight as I worked through this chapter. There are so many twists and turns, and allegiance shifts that I got lost first time through. It helped me to diagram the action. I would recommend walking through the chapter together with your student, filling in a diagram as you go. You can tell that I am definitely a visual learner, but even the non-visual types may benefit from the exercise.

2. Why was the Earl of Warwick known as the kingmaker?

3. What did Warwick mean when he said that the Duke of York's claim to the throne was a double claim? Illustrate! See the genealogy charts on pages 93 and 94.

4. How did the "Wars of the Roses" come to be called that?

5. What did Richard II do in order to gain the crown? Did his plan succeed? Explain your answer.

6. Describe Henry Tudor's ascension to the throne. How were the red and white roses united?

7. Explain the significance of the motto, "ad fontes."

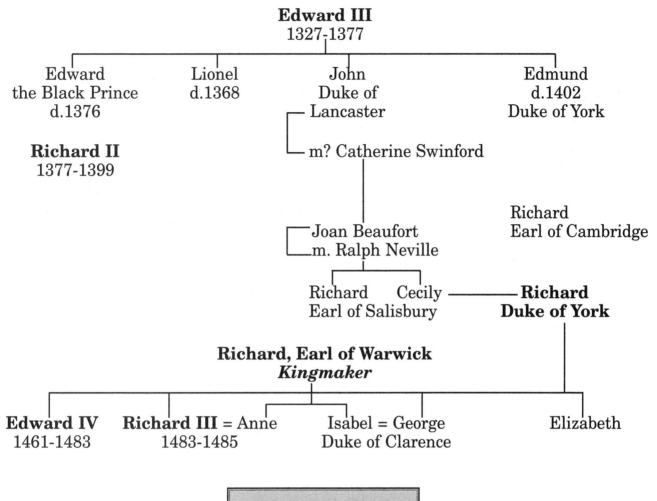

Edward III
1327-1377

Edward
the Black Prince
d.1376

Richard II
1377-1399

Lionel
d.1368

John
Duke of
Lancaster

m? Catherine Swinford

Edmund
d.1402
Duke of York

Richard
Earl of Cambridge

Joan Beaufort
m. Ralph Neville

Richard
Earl of Salisbury

Cecily ———— **Richard
Duke of York**

Richard, Earl of Warwick
Kingmaker

Edward IV
1461-1483

Richard III = Anne
1483-1485

Isabel = George
Duke of Clarence

Elizabeth

FRIENDS AND
RELATIONS
OF THE
"KINGMAKER"

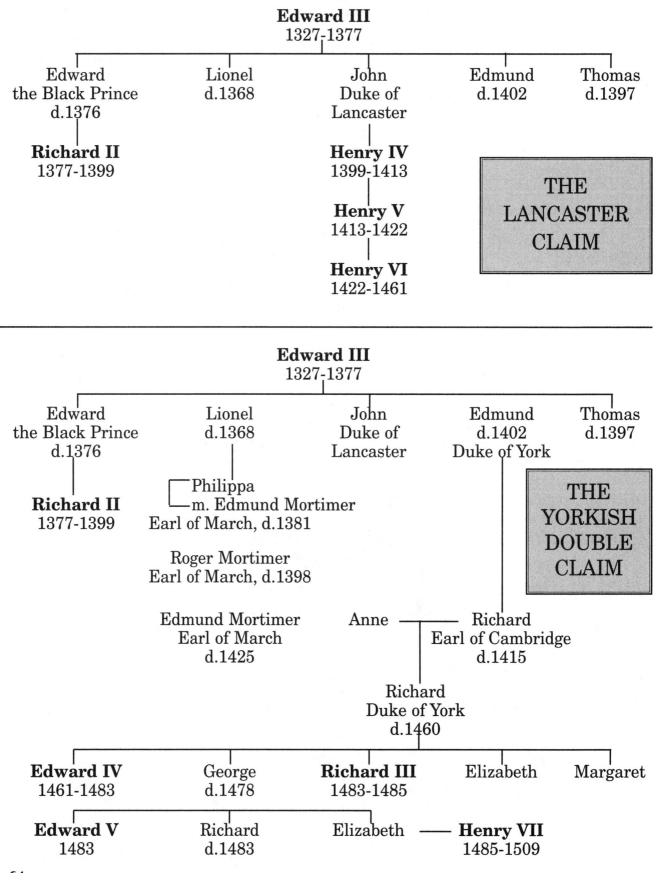

Edward III
1327-1377

Edward
the Black Prince
d.1376

Lionel
d.1368

John
Duke of
Lancaster

Edmund
d.1402

Thomas
d.1397

Richard II
1377-1399

Henry IV
1399-1413

Henry V
1413-1422

Henry VI
1422-1461

THE
LANCASTER
CLAIM

Edward III
1327-1377

Edward
the Black Prince
d.1376

Lionel
d.1368

John
Duke of
Lancaster

Edmund
d.1402
Duke of York

Thomas
d.1397

Richard II
1377-1399

Philippa
m. Edmund Mortimer
Earl of March, d.1381

THE
YORKISH
DOUBLE
CLAIM

Roger Mortimer
Earl of March, d.1398

Edmund Mortimer
Earl of March
d.1425

Anne ——— Richard
Earl of Cambridge
d.1415

Richard
Duke of York
d.1460

Edward IV
1461-1483

George
d.1478

Richard III
1483-1485

Elizabeth

Margaret

Edward V
1483

Richard
d.1483

Elizabeth —— **Henry VII**
1485-1509

A Chronology of the Middle Ages

Overview:

The Middle Ages may be grossly divided into three major periods:

500-1000	The True "Dark Ages" Roman collapse, Germanic Tribes, and Vikings
1000-1300	The High Middle Ages Knights, Castles, Cathedrals, Crusades, etc.
1300-1500	The Later Middle Ages Black Death, Hundred Years' War, War of the Roses Decline of the Church (both in morals and influence) Early Renaissance in Italy

The European culture which came to dominate in the Middle Ages, while admitting much interesting local variation, shared a common core of values and institutions. It was the result of the amalgamation of cultural inheritances from three sources: Roman, Christian, and Barbarian.

Detailed chronology:

395-455	Roman Emperors share power with their leading generals, usually Germans, such as Stilicho and Aetius.
394-410	**Alaric the Visigoth**
410	Sack of Rome by the Visigoths. The capture and pillage of the great city of Rome herself sent shock waves throughout the Empire. Many recognized that it signaled the end of Roman power.
434-453	**Reign of Attila the Hun**
427-477	**Genseric the Vandal**
429	The Roman Province of North Africa is invaded and conquered by the Vandals (led by Genseric).
455	Sack of Rome by Vandals (in a large fleet raiding from North Africa).
455-476	Germanic Emperors (such as Ricimer, Orestes, and Odoacer) rule the Western Roman Empire with ephemeral emperors as their puppets.
476 A.D.	Death of the last Roman Emperor in the West. Henceforth, Germanic generals and chieftains rule in their own name without an Emperor.
490-526	**Theodoric the Ostrogoth**
481-511	**Reign of Clovis the Frank**
496	Conversion of the Franks to Christianity
527-565	**Justinian the Great** Eastern Roman Emperor
532-534	Belisarius reconquers North Africa in the name of Justinian, the Eastern Roman Emperor.
534-554	Belisarius reconquers Italy in the name of Justinian, the Eastern Roman Emperor.

480-543	**Saint Benedict**
568	The Lombards invade and conquer Italy.
590-604	**Pope Gregory I**
570-632	**Mohammed**
632-700	Moslem Caliphate secures all of North Africa and armies cross Gibraltar into Spain. In the east, Moslem armies secure power in Palestine and Asia Minor, and begin to threaten the capital of the Eastern Roman Empire, Constantinople.
717-718	Moslem Army besieges Constantinople in the East.
732	Moslem Army defeated at Tours, France by Charles Martel. Here is a short table which summarizes the changes in major Roman provinces as they were conquered and became Germanic kingdoms. Note that Italy itself became a battleground for 300 years.
613-640	**Pepin I, Mayor of the Palace**
687-714	**Pepin II, Mayor of the Palace**

North Africa	Spain	Italy	Gaul (France)
Romans 146 BC-429 AD	Romans 20 AD-455 AD	Romans 275 BC-490 AD	Romans (Celts) 51 BC-486 AD
Vandals 429-533	Visigoths 455-711	Ostrogoths 490-554	Franks 486-today
Byzantine 533-675		Byzantine 554-568	
Moslem 675-today	Moslem 711-1492	Lombard 568-774	
		Franks 774- ??	

711-741	**Charles Martel, Mayor of the Palace**
741-768	**Pepin III, King after 751**
768-814	**Charlemagne**
774	Charlemange responds to appeals from the Pope and invades and conquers Northern Italy, ending the Lombard kingdom.
800	Charlemagne is crowned Holy Roman Emperor by Pope Leo III.
786-809	**Harun-al-Rashid, Caliph of Baghdad**
793	Sack of Lindisfarne — the traditional beginning of the Viking era from the Anglo-Saxon Chronicle, A.D. 793: "The harrying of the heathen miserably destroyed God's church in Lindisfarne by rapine and slaughter."
802-837	**Egbert the Saxon**
843	The Danish Vikings appear in force, attacking England, Ireland, and France. They raid along the English Channel, move into France and plunder Paris. A monk living at this time wrote, "The vikings overrun all that lies before them and none can withstand them.... Ships past counting voyage up the Seine, and throughout the entire region evil grows strong, and every town infested."

A Chronology of the Middle Ages
(continued)

849-901	**Alfred the Great** During the ninth century, the Danes were a particular problem to England. King Alfred (the Great) had some success in driving them back, but was not able to remove them completely. Large areas along the Eastern coast were dominated by their laws and culture, and took its name from this fact — Danelaw. By the mid 800's, some of Vikings are spending the winters in France, taking advantage of the milder weather.
845	Norwegian Vikings settle into the coasts of Ireland. They fortify a series of harbors. Remains of a Viking settlement from this period have been unearthed in Dublin.
859	Viking chiefs follow the French shoreline to the Bay of Biscay, even looting in North Africa. Then moving along the coast of Spain they circle back to France, raiding as they go. Most of the ships were lost in the three year voyage, but those who survive profit richly.
878	Treaty of Wedmore (between Alfred and the Danish Vikings) limits Danes to the Northeast portion of England (the "Danelaw").
890's	Hrolf, a Norwegian leader, arrives in the lower Seine valley.
911	King Charles the Simple, king of the Franks, formally "gives" to Hrolf the lands already in his control and gives him the title of duke. This area comes to be called Normandy from the name Hrolf's followers were known by, **Nordmanni.** Throughout the 9th and 10th centuries there are many references made to the **Rus** — a name for the Swedes that is believed to come from their name for Sweden, **Ruotsi**. The name, **Russia**, seems to be derived from this.
???-931	**Rollo the Viking**
982	Eric the Red explores Greenland.
986	Bjarni Herjulfsson sights, but does not land on the New World.
c. 1000	Leif Ericsson (Leif the Lucky) lands and attempts to colonize North America. He calls it Markland (actually Labrador). In subsequent years he attempts other settlements further south in an area he called Vinland (some think it was really Newfoundland). The settlements are occupied for only a few years. His son, Snorri was born during this time. His wife returned to Greenland at the end of the second winter. The failure of the colony is now thought to be due to conflict with the native inhabitants of the area.
979-1016	Ethelred the Unready For a time Alfred and his descendants were able to hold the Vikings at bay. With the reign of Ethelred the Unready this all fell apart. Ethelred hit upon a scheme of taxing his subjects and using the money to pay off the Vikings that were beginning to plague England again. They had returned to England and it became known that Ethelred was not the king his fathers had been. When they found that Ethelred was willing to pay them off, they came with even greater force, eager for the easy money.
1006	London Bridge is destroyed by Norwegian Vikings.

1012	Ethelred makes his last payment (Danegeld).
1013	King Swein of Denmark and his son Canute conquer England.
1014-1042	Danish rule in England
1014	Ethelred surrenders throne to Danish King Canute.
1014-1035	**Canute the Great**
1027	Canute becomes King of all England (and Denmark and Norway and part of Sweden). End of discussion over who rules England - for the moment.
1035	Canute dies. Edward the Confessor, son of Ethelred, regains throne. After a short time, Edward allows his country to be governed by the Duke of Normandy (who is a Viking descendant) so that he would be free to pursue his interest in spiritual matters. William, Duke of Normandy likes this arrangement.
mid 1000's	Harald Bluetooth brings Christianity to Denmark. Olaf the Stout brings Christianity to Norway (using the "Be Baptized or Die" school of evangelism). Christian Viking bishops (from Denmark and Norway) evangelize Sweden. Many historians believe that the Vikings' first contact had with Christianity came as they took Christian women, stolen from Ireland, into their homes as slaves.
1047	Harald Hardraada (Hard Ruler) reigns in Norway, raids in the old style throughout Scandinavia.
1035-1066	**Edward the Confessor**
1066-1087	**William the Conqueror**

1066   Death of Edward the Confessor
Following Edward's death, three men laid claim to the English throne:
    1. Earl Harold Godwinson (who was in England and half-Viking)
    2. Harald Hardraada, King of Norway and successor to Canute
    3. William of Normandy (descended from Vikings).
Harald Hardraada attacked first, and was defeated and killed by Harold Godwinson at the battle of Stamford Bridge.
William of Normandy attacked second. He defeated Godwinson's army at Hastings, killing Godwinson in the process. Henceforth he is known as William the Conqueror.

Meanwhile, back on the continent...

919-936	**Henry the Fowler**
	First of the Saxon Holy Roman Emperors (918-1024)
1040-1099	**El Cid**
1073-1085	**Pope Gregory VII**
1056-1105	**Henry IV, Holy Roman Emperor**
1076	Pope Gregory VII excommunicates Emperor Henry IV because he continues to appoint bishops without papal approval.
1077	Emperor Henry IV kneels in the snow at Canossa, begging the Pope's forgiveness.
1085	Emperor Henry IV invades Italy, besieges the Pope in Rome. Pope flees to Salerno and dies in exile.

A Chronology of the Middle Ages
(continued)

1050-1115	**Peter the Hermit**
1096-1099	The First Crusade Antioch and Jerusalem conquered in 1099.
1147-1149	The Second Crusade Unsuccessful siege of Damascus
1152-1190	**Frederick Barbarossa**
1176	Battle of Legnano, Frederick Barbarossa's allies defeated by the army of the Lombard league (who were supported by the Pope).
1187	Jerusalem reconquered by Saladin.
1187-1192	The Third Crusade "The Crusade of Kings", Frederick Barbarossa, Philip Augustus, and Richard the Lion-Hearted Acre conquered, but Jerusalem is not, Frederick Barbarossa drowns fording a river.
1154-1189	**Henry II**, King of England, Count of Anjou and Aquitaine
1170	Murder of Archbishop Thomas Beckett in Canterbury Cathedral
1189-1199	**Richard the Lion-Hearted**
1199-1216	**John Lackland**
1215	King John of England signs the Magna Carta.
1182-1226	**Saint Francis**
1170-1221	**Saint Dominic**
1202-1204	The Fourth Crusade Crusaders diverted by the Venetians to Constantinople, which falls to the crusaders in 1204.
1217-1221	The Fifth Crusade Invasion of Egypt, conquest of Damietta, followed by defeat and rout of the crusaders by Moslem army.
1215-1250	Frederick II ("Stupor Mundi" - astonisher of the world!) The Emperor who spent little time in Germany, ruled from his court in Palermo, Sicily. Fought the papacy and most Italian cities for almost all of his reign.
1228-1229	The Sixth Crusade Led by the excommunicated Frederick II who successfully negotiated access to Jerusalem for Christian pilgrims.
1226-1270	**Louis IX**
1248-1254	The Seventh Crusade Led by Louis IX, once again to Egypt. Damietta again conquered, but once again the crusaders are decisively defeated by a Moslem army.

1270	The Eighth Crusade Led by Louis IX, this time to Tunisia in N. Africa. Louis falls ill and dies, crusade abandoned.
1272-1307	Edward the First, King of England 　　Conquered Wales and added it to his kingdom. 　　Defeated the Scots and occupied Scotland. 　　Summoned the first "Parliament" in 1295.
1306-1329	**Robert Bruce**
1254-1324	**Marco Polo**
1337-1453	The Hundred Years War between England and France
1330-1376	**Edward, the Black Prince**
1337	English victory over the French at Sluys.
1346	English victory over the French at Crecy.
1347	Calais surrenders to the English.
1356	Decisive defeat of the French at Poitiers. King John of France taken prisoner and forced to cede large provinces to the English and pay a large ransom for his release.
1300-1386	**William Tell** **Arnold von Winkelried**
1333-1405	**Tamerlane**
1413-1422	**Henry V**
1412-1431	**Joan of Arc**
1415	Henry V invades France, wins a great victory at Agincourt.
1420	Treaty of Troyes Henry V marries the daughter of Charles VI of France and is named his heir. Charles VI's son (the future Charles VII) is disinherited.
1422	Henry V and Charles VI both die, leaving the French crown's proper heir much in doubt.
1422-1437	Henry V's infant son is nominally the King of both France and England, but the regency provokes power struggles between the two dynastic factions of Lancaster and York. France uses English weakness to recover most of her territory.
1429	Joan of Arc rallies the French forces of Charles VII to victory at Orleans.
1431	Joan of Arc captured, tried, and executed by the English for heresy.
1400-1468	**Gutenberg**
1428-1471	**Warwick, the Kingmaker**
1455-1485	The Wars of the Roses
1461	Edward, Duke of York seizes power from the feeble Henry VI, names himself king (with the help of Warwick the Kingmaker).
1471	Warwick switches sides and aids Henry VI in briefly regaining the throne. Edward defeats the Lancastrians at Barnet and Tewkesbury, gets the throne back.

A Chronology of the Middle Ages
(continued)

1483   Death of Edward IV. His young son is named King Edward V, with Edward's brother Richard as regent. Richard eventually deposes (and then murders his nephew?) and names himself as King Richard III.

1485   Henry Tudor, the Lancastrian heir(?) lands in England and defeats and kills Richard III at Bosworth field. Henry then married Elizabeth of York (Edward IV's daughter and Edward the V's sister) thus uniting the houses of Lancaster and York and bringing to an end the Wars of the Roses.

Student _____ Date _____

READING ASSIGNMENT CHART

Topic _____

Book Titles:

    (1)_____

    (2)_____

    (3)_____

Date	Book/Chapter	Pages

Copy as many of these as you need as you plan your study.

A Few Words About Greenleaf Press

Greenleaf Press was founded by Rob & Cyndy Shearer in 1989. It was born of their frustration in searching for a history program for their children that was at the same time challenging, interesting, and historically accurate. What they were looking for was a curriculum that would begin at the beginning and present history in a logical, readable, chronological way. None of the available, in-print programs satisfied them. They discovered that the best history books for children they could find were, sadly, out of print. The best of the out-of-print classics were really terrific. They told interesting stories about real people. And the Shearer's discovered that their children loved history when it was presented in the form of an interesting story about a real person.

And so, they founded Greenleaf Press — to bring back to life some of the wonderful biographies which had been used to teach history so successfully in the past. The reprinting of <u>Famous Men of Greece</u> and <u>Famous Men of Rome</u> were Greenleaf's first publications. Those two books have now been joined by the reprint of <u>Famous Men of the Middle Ages</u>, <u>Famous Men of the Renaissance and Reformation</u> (written by Rob Shearer), The <u>Greenleaf Guide to Old Testament History</u> (written by Rob and Cyndy Shearer), and <u>The Greenleaf Guide to Ancient Egypt</u> (written by Cyndy Shearer).

Shortly after reprinting <u>Famous Men of Rome</u>, faced with questions from many people who liked the *Famous Men* books, but wanted help in HOW to use them, they decided to publish Study Guides showing how to integrate biographies, activities, and reference material. There are *Greenleaf Guides* available for Rome, Greece, and the Middle Ages, all written by Rob & Cyndy Shearer.

From that day to this, Greenleaf Press has remained committed to "twaddle-free", living books. We believe that history is both important and exciting and that our kids can share that excitement. We believe that if our children are to understand the roots of our modern-day, mixed-up world, they must study history. We're also thoroughly convinced that studying history with our children provides us with a wonderful opportunity to reflect with them on moral choices and Godly character.

Teaching History with Greenleaf Press Curriculum

Seven Year Plan

1st Grade — *Old Testament (Historical Books: Genesis – Kings)*

2nd Grade — .... *Egypt (& Old Testament Review)*

3rd Grade — .... *Greece and Rome*

4th Grade — *The Middle Ages and The Renaissance*

5th Grade — *The Reformation and The Seventeenth Century (to 1715)*

6th Grade — *1715 to 1850*

7th Grade — *1850 to The Present*

Six Year Plan

2nd Grade — .... *Old Testament and Egypt*

3rd Grade — .... *Greece and Rome*

4th Grade — *The Middle Ages and The Renaissance*

5th Grade — *The Reformation to 1715*

6th Grade — *1715 to 1850*

7th Grade — *1850 to The Present*

Five Year Plan

3rd Grade — .... *Old Testament, Egypt, Greece & Rome*

4th Grade — *The Middle Ages and The Renaissance*

5th Grade — *The Reformation and The Seventeenth Century (to 1715)*

6th Grade — *1715 to 1850*

7th Grade — *1850 to The Present*

Four Year Plan

4th Grade — *Old Testament, Egypt, Greece & Rome*

5th Grade — *The Middle Ages, The Renaissance, and The Reformation*

6th Grade — *1600 to 1850*

7th Grade — *1850 to The Present*

Internet: www.greenleafpress.com
3761 Highway 109 N., Unit D
Lebanon, TN 37087
615-449-1617

GREENLEAF PRESS

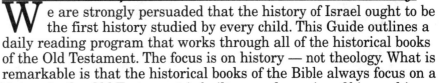

Teaching History with Living Books
An overview of
GREENLEAF PRESS
Study Guides and History Packages

The Greenleaf Guide to Old Testament History

We are strongly persuaded that the history of Israel ought to be the first history studied by every child. This Guide outlines a daily reading program that works through all of the historical books of the Old Testament. The focus is on history — not theology. What is remarkable is that the historical books of the Bible always focus on a central character. The pattern of history in the Old Testament is built around a series of biographies and character studies. The Old Testament really could be subtitled "Famous Men of Israel." Thus, the Study Guide discussion questions focus on "What actions of this person are worthy of imitation?" "What actions should we avoid?" "What is God's judgment on this life?"

The 196 readings are intended to be used, one each day throughout the school year. Yes, we know that's a few more readings than most people have school days. Be creative. You could do more than one reading on some days, or you could continue the study into the summer or the next school year. The readings are designed to give the student (and parent/teacher) an overview of the history of Israel and an introduction to the key figures whose lives God uses to teach us about Himself and His character. These stories are intended for children in the elementary grades, and should be accessible, even to children in kindergarten or first grade (though they make a rich study for older children, even teens and adults)! If this seems surprising, the reader is reminded that God's plan for families is for fathers to teach these stories to their children. When God decrees in Deuteronomy 6:6-7 that "you shall teach them diligently to your sons and shall talk of them when you sit in your house and when you walk by the way and when you lie down and when you rise up," He is not referring to math facts and grammar rules. God's textbook for children are the stories from the Old Testament. He is specifically referring to the story of the Exodus from Egypt, but by implication He means the entire Old Testament. The Old Testament is God's textbook for children. This is the only textbook, quite probably, Jesus used during his education in the house of his parents. *Duration: One full academic year*

The Greenleaf Guide to Ancient Egypt

Ever wonder how Biblical history and Ancient Egypt fit together? Why was God so angry with Pharaoh anyway? This makes a perfect second history unit for students. Or, as an alternative, you could pause in your study of Old Testament history and study Egypt after you have finished the story of Joseph at the end of the book of Genesis. This unit has ten lessons, including one devoted to the rediscovery of Egypt and the development of the science of archaeology in the 19th century. There is also a lesson on the Exodus in the context of Egyptian culture. The main text for the study is the Landmark book, The Pharaohs of Ancient Egypt, which includes biographies of the following Pharaohs:

Cheops (builder of the Great Pyramid)
Hatshepsut (His Majesty, Herself!)
Thutmose III (the Napoleon of the
  Ancient World)

Aknaton (the monotheistic Pharaoh)
Tutankamon (the boy-Pharaoh)
Rameses II (Smiter of the Asiatics)
Duration: approximately 15 weeks

Famous Men of Greece

If you were to have asked a citizen of ancient Greece to tell you something about the history of his nation, he would have wanted to begin at what he would have considered to be the beginning. He would have begun by telling you about his gods and the myths and legends told about them. Even though the events described in the myths did not actually happen in the way the story says, the Greek myths will tell you much about what was important to the people who told them.

Greek culture forms the backdrop to all the events of the New Testament. Paul was educated not just in the teachings of the Rabbis, but also in the writings of the Greeks. He was able to quote from literature in his speech to the men of Athens. Many of the details in his letters become richer and more significant when understood in the context of Greek culture.

Famous Men of Greece covers the following chapters:

Introduction: the Gods of
  Greece
Deucalion and the Flood
Cadmus and the Dragon's
  Teeth
Perseus
Hercules and His Labors
Jason and the Golden Fleece
Theseus
Agamemnon, King of Men
Achilles, Bravest of Greeks
The Adventures of Odysseus

Lycurgus
Draco and Solon
Pisistratus the Tyrant
Miltiades the Hero of
  Marathon
Leonidas at Thermopylae
Themistocles
Aristides the Just
Cimon
Pericles
Alcibiades
Lysander

Socrates
Xenophon
Epaminondas and Pelopidas
Philip of Macedonia
Alexander the Great
Demosthenes
Aristotle, Zeno, Diogenes,
  Apelles
Ptolemy
Pyrrhus
Cleomenes III
Duration: approximately 15 weeks

Famous Men of Rome

Rome was the political super-power of the ancient world. Rome history spans 500 years as a kingdom, 500 years as a Republic, and 500 years as an Empire (when Rome was ruled by military dictators who called themselves "Caesar"). It was the Pax Romana of the Empire that allowed the Gospel to spread rapidly to every corner of the earth. And it was the example of the Roman Republic which inspired the United States' Founding Fathers.

Famous Men of Rome covers the following individuals:

Romulus
Numa Pompilius
The Horatii and the Curiatii
The Tarquins
Junius Brutus
Horatius
Mucius the Left-Handed
Coriolanus
The Fabii

Cincinnatus
Camillus
Manlius
Manlius Torquatus
Appius Claudius Caecus
Regulus
Scipio Africanus
Cato the Censor
The Gracchi
Marius
Sulla
Pompey the Great

Julius Caesar
Cicero
Augustus
Nero
Titus
Trajan
Marcus Aurelius
Diocletian
Constantine the Great
End of the Western Empire

Duration: approximately 15 weeks

Famous Men of the Middle Ages

We come to a time when the power of Rome was broken and tribes of barbarians who lived north of the Danube and the Rhine took possession of the lands that had been part of the Roman Empire. These tribes were the Goths, Vandals, Huns, Franks and Anglo-Saxons. From the mixture of Roman provinces, Germanic tribes, and Christian bishops came the time known as The Middle Ages and the founding of the European nation-states.

Famous Men of the Middle Ages covers the following individuals:

The Gods of the Teutons
The Niebelungs
Alaric the Visigoth
Attila the Hun
Genseric the Vandal
Theodoric the Ostrogoth
Clovis
Justinian the Great
Two Monks: Benedict
　and Gregory
Mohammed
Charles Martel
Charlemagne
Harun-al-Rashid
Egbert the Saxon

Rollo the Viking
Alfred the Great
Henry the Fowler
Canute the Great
El Cid
Edward the Confessor
William the Conqueror
Gregory VII & Henry IV
Peter the Hermit
Frederick Barbarossa
Henry the Second and
　His Sons
Louis the Ninth
St. Francis and St. Dominic
Robert Bruce

Marco Polo
Edward the Black Prince
William Tell
Arnold Von Winkelried
Tamerlane
Henry V
Joan of Arc
Gutenberg
Warwick the Kingmaker

Duration: approximately 15 weeks (though many families supplement this study with literature readings and extend it to a full year).

Famous Men of the Renaissance and Reformation

The Middle Ages were not the "Dark Ages." Yet there had been substantial changes in Europe from 500 to 1300 AD. Rome and her Empire fell. The Germanic tribes moved into the old Roman provinces and established feudal kingdoms. Many of the Roman cities declined in population or were abandoned. Gradually, much of the literature and learning of the classical world was lost and forgotten. Around 1300, in the towns of northern Italy especially, a group of men began to devote themselves to the recovery and revival of the classical world.

As the men of the Renaissance completed their work of recovery, another group of men arose, devoted to reform of the abuses within the church and relying upon the texts and tools of scholarship developed by the Renaissance humanists. The Protestant Reformation marks the beginning of "modern" European history. During that time we see men and women of remarkable courage and ability devoted to restoring the church to Biblical patterns. There are triumphs and virtues to be imitated, and tragedies and vices to be avoided.

Famous Men of the Renaissance and Reformation covers the following individuals:

Renaissance
Petrarch
Giotto
Filippo Brunelleschi and
　Donatello
Lorenzo Valla
Cosimo D' Medici
Lorenzo D' Medici
Girolamo Savonarola
Sandro Botticelli
Leonardo Da Vinci
Cesare Borgia

Niccolo Machiavelli
Leo X (Giovanni De Medici)
Albrecht Durer
Michelangelo Buonarroti
Erasmus
Reformation
John Wyclif
Jan Hus
Martin Luther
Charles V
Ulrich Zwingli
Thomas Muntzer

Conrad Grebel & Michael
　Sattler
Melchior Hoffman, Jan
　Matthys & Menno Simons
Henry VIII
Thomas More
William Tyndale
Thomas Cromwell & Thomas
　Cranmer
John Calvin
John Knox
Duration: Approximately 15 weeks.

Graphical Timeline of Ancient History

by Robert G. Shearer
© 1996 Greenleaf Press

Key Dates

Israel
c.1900 B.C. – Joseph sold into slavery
c.1445 B.C. – The Exodus
c.1000 B.C. – Death of Saul, David becomes King
605-1344 B.C. – The Exile

Egypt
2500 B.C. – Khufu (Cheops) The Great Pyramid
1505-1484 B.C. – Queen Hatshepsut
1361-1344 B.C. – Amenhotep IV also known as Akhenaton
51-31 B.C. – Cleopatra

Greece
c.1200 B.C. – Siege of Troy
478-404 B.C. – Civil War between Athens & Sparta
356-323 B.C. – Alexander

Rome
753 B.C. – Founding of Rome
509 B.C. – Founding of the Roman Republic
100-44 B.C. – Julius Caesar
312-327 A.D. – Constantine
410 A.D. – Sack of Rome by the Visigoths
476 A.D. – Death of the last Roman Emperor

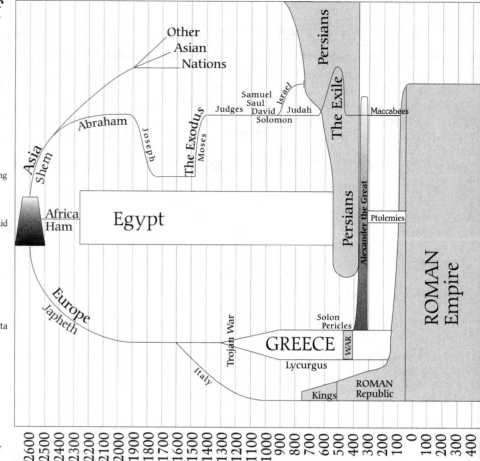

Graphical Timeline of Medieval History

Key Dates

England:
c.400 – Romans withdraw
793 – Sack of Lindisfarne by Vikings
871-899 – Alfred the Great
1066 – Norman Conquest
1339-1453 – Hundred Years War
1455-1485 – War of the Roses

France:
482-511 – Clovis
714-41 – Charles Martel
768-814 – Charlemagne
1180-1223 – Philip II Augustus
1412-1431 – Joan of Arc

Germany:
936-937 – Otto I, the Great
1152-90 – Frederick I Barbarossa
1210-50 – Frederick II, Stupor Mundi
1493-1519 – Maximilian
1516-1556 – Charles V

Italy:
440-461 – Pope Leo I
480-543 – St. Benedict
590-640 – Pope Gregory
1073-85 – Pope Gregory
1200-1240 – St. Francis
1309-1378 – Babylonian Captivity (of the Papacy)
1378-1417 – The Great Schism

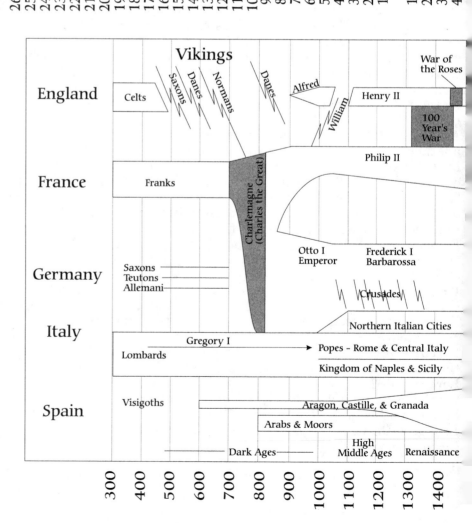